Alternative in Southeast Asia

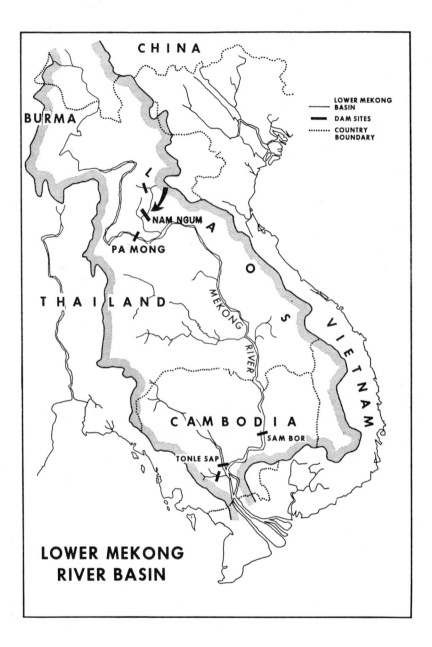

CHINA

BURMA

LOWER MEKONG
BASIN
DAM SITES
COUNTRY
BOUNDARY

L

NAM NGUM

PA MONG

THAILAND

A

O

S

VIETNAM

MEKONG RIVER

CAMBODIA

SAM BOR

TONLE SAP

**LOWER MEKONG
RIVER BASIN**

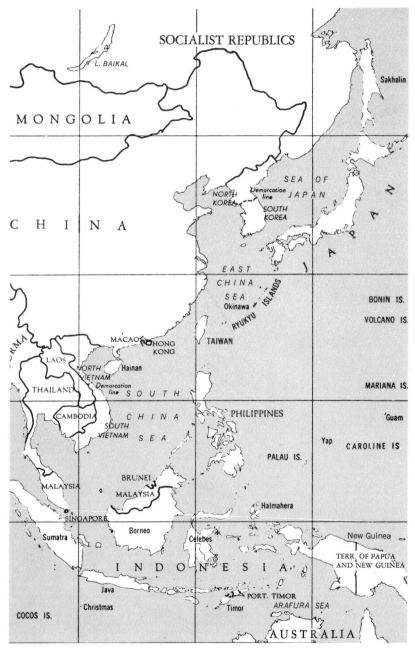

Southeast Asia, China, and Japan

Alternative in Southeast Asia

Eugene R. Black

Foreword by Lyndon B. Johnson

PALL MALL PRESS
London

Published in Great Britain in 1969 by
The Pall Mall Press Limited
5, Cromwell Place, London S.W. 7

© 1969 by Frederick A. Praeger, Inc.

SBN 269 02500 6

Printed in the United States of America

Contents

FOREWORD
by
President Lyndon B. Johnson

As part of America's effort to bring peace to Southeast Asia, I gave Eugene Black, former President of the World Bank, an important mission. His task was to encourage the nations of that area of the world to work together in a mighty venture to develop the potential resources of their region. I expressed the hope that North Vietnam would enter into "unconditional discussions" with us to end the war in Vietnam and then join and share in the regional development plan.

Hanoi rejected this invitation. It was to be three years before the discussions I sought could start, and even as I write they are still going on against a background of continued suffering in Vietnam. Mr. Black did his job as well as circumstances permitted. This book shows how he helped to lay the foundations for a new day in Southeast Asia.

In these pages, he has written not about what might have been, but about what may still be. He speaks with tremendous authority about how to substitute peaceful cooperation in development for the destruction of war. As

President of the World Bank, Mr. Black was identified with some of the most dramatic works of construction in the world—the Indus waters scheme, the re-opening of the Suez Canal after the war of 1956, the Kariba Dam in Africa. He has devoted his life to practicing what he calls "development diplomacy," the art of bringing rich and poor countries together in working accommodations designed to overcome some of the worst problems of world poverty.

He has actually been carrying on a family tradition. His grandfather, Henry Grady, the brilliant editor of the *Atlanta Constitution* in the 1880's, was known as "the architect of the New South." Henry Grady in his time did as much as anybody to heal the wounds between North and South after the Civil War. His close friend Joel Chandler Harris said of him that "he desired to be provincial in a large way, for in this country provinciality is only another name for patriotism that has taken root in rural regions." His grandson never forgets his native Georgia; to him, being "provincial in a large way" has meant carrying the message of development into the far corners of the globe.

It is a measure of Eugene Black that even after a quarter of a century of service he still is able to keep ahead of his times. Whether one agrees or not with all of his analyses and prescriptions, no reader will put this book down without being left with a whole winter's cupboard full of food for thought.

Preface

THE VIETNAM WAR has divided the generations in the
United States as has nothing else in recent history. I decided
to write this book because I believe that all those on my
side of the generation gap who have had experience in
foreign affairs have a particularly strong duty to speak out
at this time.

I am not one who leaves government service with a
burning desire to justify himself. Frankly, during the
time I served President Lyndon B. Johnson, I never knew
enough of what was going on as far as the war was
concerned to offer either a justification or a condemnation
of day-to-day policy. The reader will not find much in
this book to feed his emotions about the conduct of that
war. I was given a special task by President Johnson—to
get on with the job of planning for peace even while war
was raging at its worst. I shall always honor the President
for letting me perform this task to the best of my ability,
and I deeply believe that the instructions he gave me point

in the direction in which we must now move. However, I gladly leave it to others to fix that very big man's role in history. I am confident that the final judgment will be honorable and distinguished. All I can hope to do is draw upon my own experience to try to promote some reconciliation between the generations, insofar as their conflict affects the future conduct of foreign affairs.

When the young Americans most affected by the Vietnam war reach my venerable age, what we now call the generation gap will be a world-wide phenomenon—and very possibly a more violent phenomenon than it is today. The ideas and achievements of Western civilization have so undermined the structure and stability of every traditional society on earth that people whose immediate ancestors never dreamed of such a notion now believe that nothing's too good for the kids. They believe this because they have been convinced, essentially as a result of their numerous encounters with Western ideas and achievements, that their children will live in a world better than the one they knew. The spread of this belief lies at the root of all the promise, and all the peril, of our times.

As a representative of what might be called in Washington "the out-going generation," I am struck with the irony that, just as others are beginning to adopt the optimism and the slogans of the West, we in the West appear to have entered an age of doubt. Just as they are beginning to ride a wave of rising expectations, we are experiencing declining expectations. This is particularly so in the way we have come to regard our place in the world. The Vietnam war has left us heir to misgivings that can seriously hamper an understanding of the imperatives of foreign policy in the future. In considering what we must—or can—do now, the generation gap provides a useful point of departure. Granted that it is a silly exercise to draw lines between generations, to try to determine where one starts and another ends, I do think one can talk in a fairly precise way about a role for age and a role for youth.

Age, to be effective, must distill out of experience something called common sense. The role of age is to generalize, without hypocrisy and—as far as possible—concretely. If the generation gap is wider today in our country, wider perhaps than it has ever been, it is because age has failed to fulfill adequately its role as the articulator of common sense.

The role of youth is to discover new knowledge. Youth cannot seriously indict age except as it is able to discover new knowledge. This role is easiest to see in mathematics and the physical sciences. The wife of a close friend of mine, herself a mathematician, tells me that in her profession the really creative years usually come between twenty and thirty. That is when most new mathematical knowledge is discovered. Her observation seems to apply as well to the physical sciences and to be borne out by the youthful ages of many scientists who have recently won Nobel prizes.

But the important new knowledge youth is discovering today has to do with the human condition. If I read correctly the indictment that youth levels against age, it is largely concerned with the easy generalizations we have come to use in talking about such things as the brother-hood of man, equality between the races and the sexes, or law and order, or international cooperation and peace among nations. What passed even a short time ago as sensible talk about these matters no longer washes with the younger generation. The theologian Paul Tillich once observed that there is no reality without an accompanying belief. And it is the beliefs—the philosophy, if you will—of age that are under attack all over the world today.

In these brief essays, I have tried to examine some con-ventional beliefs about world affairs and, in the process, test my own. I have tried to distill a common-sense ap-proach to our future relationships with the countries of Southeast Asia. Not being a scholar myself, I have bor-rowed freely from many distinguished scholars (but spared them any danger of guilt by association by not footnoting all that I have borrowed). I would like to mention espe-cially my indebtedness to Bernard Gordon, of the Johns Hopkins School for Advanced International Studies, for letting me see in advance portions of this book *Toward Disengagement in Asia: A Strategy for American Foreign*

Policy (Englewood Cliffs, N.J.: Prentice-Hall, 1969), and to Theodore Geiger, Director of International Studies at the National Planning Association in Washington, whose book *The Conflicted Relationship: The West and the Transformation of Asia, Africa, and Latin America* (New York: McGraw-Hill, 1967) has challenged my thinking on many occasions since it was published.

I am particularly grateful to Thomas Niblock, Director of East Asian Regional Affairs, Agency for International Development, not only for making available to me large amounts of documentation, but also for giving me such tireless and dedicated guidance during my tour of work for President Johnson. I also wish to thank Lois Decker O'Neill, Washington editor for Frederick A. Praeger, Publishers, who suggested that three lectures I delivered at Emory University, in Atlanta, Georgia, be expanded to make this book. Finally, I am indebted to my associate of many years' standing, Nathaniel McKitterick, and his research assistant, Mary Laird, for helping me to put these thoughts in order.

EUGENE R. BLACK

New York City
June, 1969

Alternative in Southeast Asia

I

A New Diplomacy for Southeast Asia

LAST YEAR, Hans J. Morgenthau, perhaps the most serious critic of President Johnson's Vietnam policy, wrote in *The New Republic* that "a nation which refuses to accept the primacy of foreign policy over domestic politics has doomed itself." [*]

Professor Morgenthau was here arguing against those who urged the President to wash his hands of the war in Vietnam on the grounds that, given the serious development problems in urban areas at home, the United States could no longer afford the expense of its military commitment. To him, this was the least acceptable of all criticisms. Either the war reflected a real national interest of the United States or it did not; it should not be judged on the basis of its material cost, nor even its human cost, but on the basis of the national purposes it was designed to serve.

In this regard, I am in agreement with Professor

[*] Hans J. Morgenthau, "Bundy's Doctrine of War Without End," *The New Republic,* November 2, 1968, p. 20.

Morgenthau. Foreign policy must be judged in relation to the national interests it is designed to serve. And, if our nation is to survive, those interests must be primary. It is the most dangerous of illusions to believe that, because science and technology have made it possible for men and nations to liberate themselves from lives of drudgery, men and nations can also think in terms of liberating themselves from the vast forces of history that circumscribe our security.

Many Americans, Professor Morgenthau among them, are not persuaded that our military involvement in Vietnam was necessary for our national security or conducive to preventing World War III. But only future historians can pass definitive judgment on those questions. To me, what is important now is to define anew our national interest in Southeast Asia and devise policies designed to serve that interest. So much bitterness and confusion have been generated over the war itself that America is in grave danger of ignoring its real interests in favor of licking its wounds.

Before we try to fashion a new definition, however, I think it is important to try also to understand why we Americans seem to have such singular difficulty describing, even to ourselves, what our real interests in the world are.

The Moral and Rational Dimensions of Policy

I have the impression that rather more scholarship is devoted to how other societies see their place in the world than to how we see our place. One reason, perhaps, is that Americans suffer from a historical confusion over rational and moral arguments when addressing world problems. John Winthrop, first Governor of the Massachusetts Bay Colony, may have started the confusion when he likened America to a "city upon a hill," a shining demonstration that the elect of God were creating in the wilderness a society that would serve as a moral example to all mankind. At any rate, ever since the days of our Puritan forebears, Americans have tended to look at the world not as it is but as we think it ought to be.

The moral dimension always present in our foreign policy was greatly strengthened as we learned to harness the forces of nature and to create in our own society the greatest reservoir of material wealth man has ever known. Even in our isolationist days, our foreign policy was morally aggressive; American politicians stood willing to judge the rights and wrongs of world conflicts, to tell other countries how they should act, and to offer their services as arbiters and mediators, even while stoutly resisting any and all political involvement. They were permitted this luxury, of course, because America's real interests for the most part were pretty well defended by the British fleet.

World War II propelled us out of our self-righteous isolation, but we were still quite unprepared for our subsequent postwar involvement, as the world's most powerful international force, in the affairs of others.

Faced with a quantum jump in military power, represented by the development of nuclear weapons, and a quantum jump in human expectations, represented by the fantastic impact on traditional societies and colonial territories of Western technological achievements, Western economic penetration, and Western ideas of participatory government, we have had to learn to live in an uncomfortable intimacy with the rest of the world and to contend with the turbulent result of our heritage while acting as the primary agent for keeping the peace. Fortunately, in my view, we did not in this difficult period after World War II abandon the now secularized moral dimension in our foreign policy. Indeed, we underlined our moral purposes through such acts as taking leadership in the formation of the United Nations and mounting a large and continuing foreign aid program. I say "fortunately" because I believe that this planet would be an even more dangerous and troubled place than it is today if the United States had not leavened its foreign policy with generous servings of humanitarianism. Without a vision of world order, of progressive disarmament, of a world in which law has some truly international significance and force, each succeeding generation would be doomed to increasing cynicism.

Unfortunately, however, our involvement in world affairs inevitably brought with it the agony of having to set priorities and limits on our commitments, despite our wealth and strength. We have had to sharpen the rational arguments in our foreign policy and temper our moral pretensions. We have had to learn to understand Reinhold Niebuhr's profound insight that "ideals, to be effective, must be rooted in interests."

More than anything else in modern American history, the Vietnam war underlines the importance of this insight. If we regard that war, as some do, solely in its moral dimension (as though wars could ever be justified morally in our time), we are in for serious trouble. Perhaps the greatest danger in relying too heavily on moral justifications in the determination of foreign policy is that, when things go wrong, as they inevitably will, the natural tendency is to blame others, not ourselves. I find very unwise the strain of criticism of the war that tends to blame all our difficulties on an imputed corruption or venality among those in South Vietnam, particularly in the government, with whom we have been working most closely. This criticism starts with an assumption of lofty moral purpose on our part but degenerates into something very like racism.

In the 1950's, Americans bitterly debated "who lost China?" on the fantastic assumption that China used to be "ours." One group of critics assaulted the diplomatic service of the United States with wild charges of treason. Another blackened the reputations of those Chinese alongside whom we had worked and fought. It was one of the least edifying periods of American history. If we have not learned since then the grave dangers of trying to explain important historical developments in terms of other peoples' imputed immorality, we will surely manufacture our own defeat in Vietnam.

More than anything else, it is the moral pretensions of the Communists that have brought to the fore our own deep confusion over moral and rational arguments in foreign policy. If there is any validity to the idea of peaceful or competitive coexistence of Communist and non-Communist states—and I believe there is—it must rest on the belief that rational arguments will inhibit both sides. We will temper the moral pretensions of the Communists not by crusading but by dealing with their threats pragmatically and by stressing the fact that no intelligent man any longer believes that moral questions can be settled on the battlefield.

It was inevitable I think, that we would treat the world Communist movement as a single threat so long as the power came from one center, dominated by a man like Josef Stalin. But it has become self-defeating for Americans to continue to lean on this image of monolithic Communism long after the power realities have changed. Ten years ago, in addressing a group of students at Oxford University in England, I said:

> Capitalists, of whom I consider myself one, have come in a great many shapes and sizes for a great many years now. Should we not be proud of this diversity and lay stress upon it? And while we are at it, can we not say that

Communists, too, are beginning to appear in a few different shapes and sizes? Shouldn't we also stress this? After all, the quest for peace demands that the Communists be encouraged to shed their illusions about the nature of competition among nations, even as we shed ours.

In the ten years since I made those remarks, the fragmentation of world Communism has progressed a great deal further. We are not serving our own interests, much less the cause of world peace, by asserting that the peasant guerilla in the Vietnamese jungle has an ideology in common with the Cuban revolutionary or the Russian worker. Surely it is misplaced evangelism to use our power and influence in a way that creates common ground among the increasingly disparate groups who call themselves Communists. Yet we are always in danger of doing just that when we permit the moral dimension to overwhelm the rational dimension in foreign policy, when we are tempted anew to anti-Communist crusades.

This is not to say that the United States should abandon its sense of mission in the world. Most Americans involved in foreign operations are to some degree missionaries. We could not deny this quality in ourselves even if we wanted to—and we should not want to. The world is fascinated by, and wants to learn from, our manifold achievements. We will always exert an influence whether we try to do so deliberately or choose to remain aloof.

But, as Paul Tillich has written, good missionaries know

that their moral view is only one possible expression, and that it is certain to be tentative and transitory. A nation that believes its moral view is the only reality can only be a threat to the peace of the world.

OUR NATIONAL INTEREST IN SOUTHEAST ASIA

The American's historical confusion over the difference between rational and moral dimensions in foreign policy has contributed importantly to making the Vietnam war such a divisive event in our country. For whether or not one agrees with the size and character of our military investment in Vietnam, the investment *was* made in pursuit of an important national interest. One may argue over the degree of importance of that interest. One may even argue that we would have been better served if we had not gone to war. But no impartial critic can deny its existence. In Vietnam and Southeast Asia in general that interest is to prevent the domination of Asia by a single power.

Before World War II, Japan threatened to dominate Asia. Today, China poses that threat.

I am aware that the immediacy of the Chinese threat to Southeast Asia is argued heatedly in professional circles. There are those who say that Chinese domination of the region is inevitable, no matter what we do, and those who say that it is a very remote threat both because of the current weakness of China and because of the essential indigestibility of the nations making up Southeast Asia.

Others say that the Vietnamese are the traditional enemies of the Chinese, and that we have therefore erred tragically by involving ourselves in a war between two factions of Vietnamese, even though one is a Communist faction. Still others see in the ambitions of Communist North Vietnam and Communist China parallel and mutually re-enforcing threats, which mean that if either were to succeed both would be encouraged and the will and ability of other nations in the region to resist domination would be correspondingly reduced.

I am not competent to judge the merits of these competing and conflicting views, but common sense suggests that it would be rash, on the basis of scholarly evidence available, to minimize our national interest in preventing one country from dominating Southeast Asia. I can report that men like Prime Minister Lee Kwan Yew of Singapore, Prime Minister Tunku Abdul Rahman of Malaysia, Foreign Minister Thanat Khoman of Thailand, and Prince Souvanna Phouma, Premier of Laos, do not in any way minimize the immediacy of the Chinese threat. Nor do the people of South Korea. Had they done so they would not have supported the United States in the war in Vietnam as they have. Even Prince Sihanouk of Cambodia, whose dedication to Cambodian independence has kept him determinedly neutral, makes no bones about the fact that if the United States withdraws from Southeast Asia, his country will forthwith come under Chinese domination.

I realize that there are those who ask, "So what? What difference does it make to the United States if China simply absorbs all of Southeast Asia?" Many who make this point are too young to remember that in 1941 the militarist leaders of Japan decided to bomb Pearl Harbor because they knew that the United States had a serious national interest in preventing Japanese domination of East Asia and thought—though they were terribly wrong—that they could inhibit our response by their action. Those who believe that this kind of mistake cannot happen again in this century, under Chinese instigation, are, I am afraid, guilty of the most dangerous kind of wishful thinking. History offers no encouragement to those who hold that the existence of nuclear weapons means that imperial ambitions have become obsolete. Indeed, the authorities in Peking are often at pains to remind us that this is not so.

Finally, there is the view that it is more important to grant diplomatic recognition to China and to normalize relations in some manner than it is to follow any particular policy in Southeast Asia. This argument is warmly supported by many who remember our former friendship with the Chinese people and yearn for a return to those days. It is supported, too, by those who hope that we can use our influence with Peking to widen the split between China and Russia.

Nothing better illustrates our failure to distinguish

between moral and rational arguments than the importance we have attached to diplomatic recognition as an instrument of policy. I certainly favor establishing direct diplomatic links with Peking, if we can, and accepting Communist China into the United Nations—provided, of course, that the independence and integrity of Taiwan are maintained, since we have both a rational and a moral interest in Taiwan's independence and subordination of these interests to diplomatic recognition of Peking would be disastrous. The policy of nonrecognition appears to me to have lost whatever diplomatic usefulness it may have had in the past. But I am mystified by those who think a change to a policy of recognition will, in and of itself, have much result, even if the terribly difficult Chinese puzzles of U.N. representation and continued independence of Taiwan can be solved.

As for our friendship for the people of China, we certainly cannot restore former harmony by ignoring our own interests in East Asia. Red China is one of the biggest facts in the modern world. The evolution of that nation of about 750 million will, without doubt, determine in a significant way the future of mankind. We must do what we can to influence that evolution in directions compatible with our own security and well-being—and preventing Chinese domination of Southeast Asia is a necessary, unavoidable step if we are to gain time in which to exert such influence.

It is only common sense, I think, to expect that because of the threat of Chinese domination we will have to maintain a military presence of some kind in East Asia for many years to come. We still have two divisions in Korea nearly fifteen years after the cessation of hostilities there. I wager that we will have to keep a comparable force in or around Vietnam for at least as long. Not to do so would be to risk destroying the most important element making for peace in the area, namely, credibility in the effectiveness of American military power, and in the willingness of the U.S. Government to commit that power to prevent any one nation from dominating the region.

The Limits of U.S. Power

What is new about the world today is not a decline in imperial ambitions, but a divergence between the military power and the political influence of the superpowers, Russia and the United States.

After World War II, the heightened sense of national and personal power attendant upon the development of nuclear weapons encouraged important people, in both the United States and Russia, to think that together or separately the two nations would have an influence in the world commensurate with their great military power. Some Americans thought briefly that peace and order could be maintained after World War II through successive Soviet-American agreements. Vital parts of the U.N.

Charter were designed with this thought in mind. However, as we all know, things fell out differently. Stalin saw himself as head of a unified, world-wide Communist movement, bound to intervene in the affairs and development of countries outside Russia's immediate sphere. Americans saw themselves as uniquely equipped and morally obligated not just to oppose Stalin's designs, but to provide the resources and the resourcefulness needed to manage the complex processes of economic growth and political modernization that had set in throughout most of Asia, Africa, and Latin America.

With the benefit of hindsight, it is easy to understand why both the Russian and the American strategies of massive intervention were destined to lead to disillusionment and disappointment for their promoters. Many barely viable nations, dependent on outside resources for security and growth, naturally bitterly resented such dependence as a threat to their national integrity. Gradually, these nations have devised ways and means of neutralizing some of the ill effects of intervention while retaining some of the rewards. They have been able to embrace a self-righteous policy of nonalignment because of the standoff between the nuclear superpowers, much as the United States was once able to indulge a self-righteous isolationism in the shelter of the British fleet.

Although the balance of terror has so far persuaded both the United States and Russia that no intervention is worth a direct confrontation between them, intervention goes on apace—not just on the part of the United States and Russia, but increasingly on the part of China as well. Intervention will be inevitable as long as the superpowers believe a vital national interest is at stake and as long as so many nations in the world need external support. No longer, however, can innocence protect the United States from the consequences of such intervention. Our influence, as well as Russia's, has plainly diverged from our power and probably will diverge even more as parts of Asia, Africa, and Latin America erupt in periodic chaos and revolution. The problem for the United States today is not to eschew intervention, but to make sure that its essays at intervention, as well as its ideals, are grounded in real interests.

The most telling criticism of the Vietnam war, I think, has come from those who have acknowledged the fact of aggression and the need for the United States to take action to stop it but at the same time have argued that it was quite impossible either to restore internal stability in South Vietnam with the use of our armed forces or, in the presence of our armed forces, to promote genuine self-determination. It was right, these critics say, to fight to preserve the possibility of self-determination, wrong to pretend that self-determination would be possible so long as the American presence remained as heavy and all-pervasive as it has.

A tacit acknowledgment of our inability to promote, by ourselves, genuine self-determination and internal stability in South Vietnam has been implicit throughout the peace talks that began in Paris in the spring of 1968. I think that before beginning to chart an alternative course in Southeast Asia it is important to make explicit what this acknowledgment means.

PROGRAMMED DEVELOPMENT AND COUNTERINSURGENCY

Beyond the simple fact of aggression, our deep intervention in the domestic affairs of South Vietnam was sustained by two doctrines. The first I think of as the doctrine of "programmed development." The second is recognized within government as the doctrine of counterinsurgency. Programmed development was designed to win what the newspapers call the battle for men's minds by combining our own and South Vietnam's economic resources to bring about a rapid rise in living standards. The second involved using our military and paramilitary forces, as well as our economic resources, to help maintain internal security and political stability. Under pressure from the Department of Defense, these two doctrines came together to be acted out in the Agency for International Development (AID). The agency, in effect, was South Vietnam's major banker during the war.

Both doctrines proved faulty in Vietnam and, in the process, helped to destroy much public and professional support for the whole idea of foreign aid. Since I believe that the most logical, acceptable, and necessary form of intervention in the world today is foreign aid—or development finance as I prefer to call it—I cannot but feel very strongly that the damage done to our foreign aid agency by the war in general and by these two doctrines in particular must be repaired.

Both the doctrine of counterinsurgency and what I call the doctrine of programmed development were utopian in conception. They are, unfortunately, excellent examples of the perennial American tendency to see the world, not as it is, but as we think it ought to be.

The most damaging of the two has been counterinsurgency—the 1960's sequel to the anti-Communist crusade of the 1950's. Its doctrinaire supporters claimed that the United States could defeat Communist-led "wars of national liberation" wherever they broke out. Unfortunately, their premise suffered, among other things, from the same major flaw that afflicted the anti-Communist crusade of the previous decade: it ignored the fact that influence was no more commensurate with power in the Communist world than in our own and that, accordingly, the real interests of the United States were certain to demand different responses in different situations.

The doctrine of counterinsurgency assumed also that the United States and the governments that it was helping had progressive, if not revolutionary, programs of their own with which to counter the propaganda of those who led the wars of national liberation. When this turned out not to be so—in Latin America as well as in South Vietnam—counterinsurgency became little more than a vehicle with which to support the *status quo* or prevent radical change.

As far as I know, programmed development has never been formally enunciated as a doctrine by any leading scholar or official, although the conception is suggested by Walt W. Rostow's thesis in *The Stages of Economic Growth* (New York: Cambridge University Press, 1960). Nonetheless, in the minds of some officials the idea of programmed development sometimes appeared as the means by which counterinsurgency could be justified. Equating development with economic growth (an assumption that I hope to show is a fundamental fallacy), it held that the United States could program its foreign aid funds with the economic resources of other governments to bring about rapid, if not radical, change in the social as well as the economic environment in other countries. In actual operations, programmed development has never really been so implemented. However, the growing dominance of the economist in the councils of AID and in the literature of development in general, together with the prominence of the doctrine of counterinsurgency within the U.S. Government, created the widespread impression that American officials thought that "development" could be "programmed" in such a way that official U.S. actions would bring about revolutionary changes.

This impression pervades the literature of the Alliance for Progress, for example, implying that through joint programming of local economic resources and foreign aid, the goals of the Punta del Este Charter would be realized. There has not been anything like the professional analysis necessary for a sound judgment of the contribution to development that has been made under the Alliance for Progress. However, I have the feeling that while there may have been considerable economic growth in Latin America, those closest to the program are disappointed that so little progress has been made toward some of the Charter's goals. Perhaps that is because the Charter's goals are not really economic goals, and because things like social justice, efficient tax systems, and participatory government do not spring automatically from economic growth. What is undeniably true is that there have not been any revolutions of consequence in Latin America during the span of the Alliance, despite the very revolutionary rhetoric of those who promoted the idea in the first place.

I for one am not at all sure that it is in the interests of the United States to pretend, through official rhetoric or otherwise, that we seriously want to promote revolutions outside our country. I have never understood how the United States can hope to play such a role successfully—nor why it should. We approach our own economic and social problems (our at-home development problems, if you will) pragmatically. Why not urge others to do the same? Instead, when it comes to articulating foreign policy, we seem impelled to leave the arguments of pragmatism at the water's edge.

Intervention against the threat of Communist political subversion (as opposed to direct aggression) demands a pragmatic response. Often, it may not be in our interests to intervene at all. At other times, a pragmatic use of our resources for military and paramilitary training and for budgetary support in emergency situations may be necessary. In any case, it is of paramount importance that the justification for intervention not rest on utopian doctrines or mistaken notions about the process we call development. For when these doctrines prove inadequate, as they have in Vietnam, the moral purposes of the United States, as well as its legitimate national interests, suffer through the loss of public support and understanding here at home. This is the real tragedy of the Vietnam war.

Toward a New Policy

Economics and political science may be essential tools of analysis in the fashioning of effective foreign policy, but, like any tools, they can be used or misused. In the conduct of foreign policy, they are much more likely to be misused if they are not subjected to the disciplines of that ancient art called diplomacy. If the United States is to avoid isolationism, on the one hand, and an insupportable role as the world's policeman, on the other, we have no choice, in my opinion, but to revive and cultivate anew that art.

Unhappily, in the United States the word diplomacy has lost its standing—and not without good reason. During World War II, President Franklin D. Roosevelt in effect classified the Department of State and the Foreign Service of the United States as 4-F. He was aware that the prewar Foreign Service had crippled itself by committing a grave error: instead of exercising leadership in the making of foreign policy, it had rested content to reflect the isolationism that was certainly the dominant view of the American people. President Roosevelt knew that public opinion by itself is not a sufficient guide for the formulation of foreign policy and that, vital as public support and understanding may be, the people cannot lead in its making.

As Professor Morgenthau says, a nation dooms itself if it applies to the formulation of foreign policy the same priorities that it applies to the formulation of domestic policies. The framers of our Constitution fully recognized this when they vested the authority for the formulation and conduct of foreign policy in the Presidency rather than in the Congress. The trouble is that the State Department and the Foreign Service of the United States have never really been reclassified since the end of World War II.

Since FDR's day, our diplomatic bureaucracy has under-
gone a seemingly unending series of vivisections. Leadership is now divided amongst what one government report
calls "a family of foreign services." Of the dozens of
reports on the role and organization of the State Department since World War II, not one has failed to express
stern disapproval of "the old diplomacy." Ironically,
however, not one, to my knowledge, has ascribed its weakness to a too close adherence to prevailing public opinion
at home or recognized that its real failure was its too
ready acceptance of the conventional, popular view of the
world prevailing in the United States.

Since World War II, the Foreign Service of the United
States, as a professional service, has had a remarkably small
role in the formulation of policy on many important occasions. Despite the personal involvement of distinguished
and able individuals, the State Department as such played
second fiddle to the military in the formulation of policy
in Vietnam in the years between Diem's overthrow and
the Paris peace talks. The Department was caught by
surprise when the North Koreans invaded South Korea
in 1950, and it had little or nothing to do with the episode
at the Bay of Pigs.

What the United States has done is to give over much
of the conduct of diplomacy and of foreign policy formulation to amateurs. I myself am an amateur. We amateurs
can be very effective, very wise, very useful on occasion,

but we are not a substitute for a professional diplomatic service, charged with an important role in the formulation of foreign policy. And because we have no allegiance to such a service, we usually contribute nothing more lasting to diplomacy than what is involved in an *ad hoc* assignment. In the process, we often need an unconscionable amount of on-the-job training.

Even in the academic community, the word diplomacy has fallen out of fashion. It has been replaced by such phrases as "international relations." International relations is sometimes taught as a degree study. Diplomacy as such is not—and an understanding of the art of diplomacy seems to play a very small part in the study of international relations. Academicians move freely in and out of diplomatic posts, but like the rest of us amateurs, their allegiance is to something else—to their universities or to a discipline, be it economics or political science or some other—rather than to a professional diplomatic service. It is certainly true that diplomacy today needs to be informed to a much greater degree than ever before by such new knowledge as the academic world can produce, but the academic world, at the same time, needs to show a much greater appreciation of what diplomacy is all about.

It is within the bureaucracy, however, that the situation is most serious. Here diplomacy has yielded again and again to something known as "crisis management." Diplomats, who should be concerned with heading off crises before they are on top of us, have been all too willing to take a back seat in favor of practitioners of counterinsurgency, development programmers, propaganda engineers, and a host of others. In the State Department, as in television, the media have triumphed over matter. Overseas, our ambassadors, even where they have established command over large American bureaucratic enclaves, have had to become business managers, rather than skilled analysts of the local political scene and effective advocates of American interests. Every President and every Secretary of State since World War II has suffered from the lack of a single, highly professional diplomatic service. None has been free enough from crises to do anything much about the situation.

In 1968, a group of "Young Turks" in the American Foreign Service Association (AFSA) organized to bring about reform in what I think is the only realistic way possible: that is, from within the Foreign Service itself. The major plank in the AFSA's program is the establishment of a single, professional service with clear norms and duties and control over its own training and personnel policies. It is going to take a long time to bring about this much needed reform, for there are in the government many with vested interests opposed to such a change. I hope, however, that the ASFA's objective receives from the Congress and from President Nixon the high priority it deserves. I especially hope that the relevant congressional committees will take the problems of the Foreign Service seriously, for it is a characteristic of an effective government service, with a high *esprit de corps,* that it has close and friendly working relations with its parent committees in the Congress. The cessation of hostilities in Vietnam will give both Congress and the executive branch of our government a rare opportunity to re-establish diplomacy as the real specialty in foreign affairs, with all other activities simply subdivisions of diplomatic labor.

In subsequent chapters, I will give many illustrations of what I mean by cultivating anew the arts of diplomacy. In chapters IV, V, and VI, I will show how I think that the special business of development finance should be related to professional diplomacy. But a serious discussion of future policies in Southeast Asia should start, in my opinion, by first recognizing the primacy of diplomacy.

This order of importance is very hard, I know, for Americans to accept. Americans are activists. We believe in the redeeming qualities of action in a way no other society ever has. Our enormous energy and inventiveness are perhaps our greatest strength. But mere actions can never be a substitute for diplomacy. In fact, one of the continuing, thankless tasks of American diplomats will always be to curb the activist instincts of their too eager fellow countrymen. This can only be done by a highly professional diplomatic service, capable of helping the President to define clearly and persuasively the real national interests of our country in the world and effective at helping to formulate policies to serve those interests.

POLICY IN A MULTILATERAL FRAMEWORK

I emphasize the vital importance of cultivating and understanding the diplomatic arts because, looking ahead in Southeast Asia, I see only one course consistent with our real interests, and such a course is going to demand of us a skill in diplomatic navigation that we have rarely exhibited in our relations with Asia. In the wake of a cessation in hostilities in Vietnam, I think we will have to substitute for an overwhelming American presence a multilateral framework for our policy. This alternative is much easier to prescribe than to carry out.

Our presence in Vietnam has not been quite as unilateral as we here at home have come to think. Korea, Thailand, Australia, New Zealand, and the Philippines have all made important contributions, military and otherwise. However, in contrast to the Korean war, in which we acted with the sanction of the United Nations and with active support from our European allies and, so far as supplies were concerned, from Japan as well, we can be said to have been "going it alone" in Vietnam. This has been the case in part because many of our allies simply did not see a national interest of their own at stake, in part because some actively opposed our interests, and in part because we made it so clear that we were going to take all the important responsibilities that others undoubtedly felt they did not have to participate. In various ways, the reactions of our European allies and Japan to our involvement in Vietnam have been good evidence of how far our military and economic power and our real influence in world affairs have diverged.

Part of the case for casting our policy in a multilateral framework is the need to bring back into effective and constructive participation in the affairs of Southeast Asia important nations, particularly Japan, which have both the resources and, logically, the national interests to make an effective contribution, first to reconstruction and development, and later to the security of the area. It is going to be a difficult and delicate task to stimulate multilateral action, especially in the case of Japan, as I shall try to illustrate in Chapter III. However, the surest way to prevent such action is for the United States to attempt to do too much itself. The day has long passed when we could hope to play coach in world affairs and assign plays and positions to even our closest allies.

The focus of a multilateral policy in Southeast Asia must be, I think, that most difficult of all objectives, regional cooperation. No nation has preached regional cooperation more often and more passionately since World War II than has the United States. Americans played a big part in establishing the regional branches of the United

Nations—the economic commissions in Europe (ECE), in Latin America (ECLA), in Asia (ECAFE), and in Africa (ECA). In the Marshall Plan days, Americans took many initiatives leading to the establishment of regional institutions in Western Europe. The same has been true of the recent history of regionalism in Latin America. Only in the Arab world have we failed to help plant at least the bare beginnings of regional institutions.

In a lecture at Leeds University in England in 1967, Walt W. Rostow summed up succinctly that common thread of national interest which led the United States to champion regionalism in so many places:

> Regionalism—in Western Europe and elsewhere—has . . . commended itself to the United States as a way of permitting us to shift away from the disproportionate bilateral relations inherent in a large power working with smaller powers. We see in regionalism a way of *not* returning to isolationism, but of leaving the nations of the various regions to do as much for themselves as they can— and more with the passage of time—while preserving the ties of interdependence where they are judged on both sides to be in the common interest.*

Unfortunately, we have not always been modest in our pursuit of regionalism. In particular, we have not realized

---

* W. W. Rostow, "The Great Transition: Tasks of the First and Second Post-War Generations," *The Twenty-fifth Montague Burton Lecture on International Relations* (Leeds University Press, 1967), p. 19.

that our interests in promoting regionalism are not exactly the same in every region. In Latin America, for example, we are not concerned with preventing the domination of the region by a single power, as we are in Southeast Asia, Western Europe, and the Middle East. Since the Monroe Doctrine, our policies in Latin America have contained within them the premise that we wish to preserve our own benevolent dominance in the hemisphere. This premise is one reason why our sponsorship of regionalism in Latin America has yielded such meager results in comparison with, say, our policy in Western Europe. For the opposite reason, since our national interests in Africa are, for the most part, minimal, our sponsorship of regionalism there has also yielded next to no results.

Regionalism is more important to us in Southeast Asia precisely because it does reflect a real national interest of ours and because the possibility exists for pursuing that interest in ways compatible with the interests of the governments of Southeast Asia as those governments see them. Given the belligerent diversity of Southeast Asia, it is easy to dismiss this possibility as wishful thinking. The "objective facts" as set forth by economists and political scientists seem to make a mockery out of all facile plans for institutionalizing regional cooperation on the European or Latin American models. However, as I hope to show in the next chapter, it is the very diversity of the region that makes it practical to talk of regional cooperation.

Later chapters suggest the kinds of institutions that we may be able to help the governments of Southeast Asia establish and build upon over time.

The policy I sketch is not dramatic. It is certainly no panacea. It may only point toward an escape from our present predicament into one with which we can live more easily and constructively. But that in itself seems to me a fairly precise definition of progress. And if we would disentangle ourselves from our confusion over the moral and the rational arguments in foreign policy, we could, I am sure, find in this alternative not just a lot of exciting work to do, but also a way of preserving our ideals through work, thereby justifying our deep belief in the redemptive power of action.

II

Regional Cooperation: Absurd or Inevitable?

THERE ARE such formidable and divisive cultural, historical, and economic forces at work within the nations of Southeast Asia that many scholars dismiss the idea of regional cooperation as absurd. Some even deny that Southeast Asia can be treated usefully as a region, so great is the diversity of its peoples and their interests.

Between the large, offshore archipelagoes of Indonesia and the Philippines and the arc of mainland nations stretching from Burma to Vietnam, there are not today any close ties—nor have there been in recent centuries. Among the cluster of mainland nations, there is a history of conflict between races and communities that goes back many centuries.

However, despite all that militates against regional cooperation, the subject has become ever more prominent in the pronouncements of Southeast Asian leaders. It is treated more seriously in Djakarta and Bangkok and the other capitals of the area than it is in Washington, and discussion of it has grown livelier as more and more leaders, watching our reactions to our unhappy experience in Vietnam, have become concerned over the future intentions of the United States.

Any appraisal of the prospects for regional cooperation must first try to reconcile these apparent contradictions.

A BELLIGERENT DIVERSITY, A COMMON EXPERIENCE

The able journalist Sol Sanders says in his recent book *A Sense of Asia* (Scribners, New York: 1969) that it is better to talk of Southeast Asia as a complex of countries rather than as nations, as we use the term in the West. More often than not, allegiances are still centered on the extended family or the village, instead of on a nation or any particular government; these very particular allegiances in some ways suggest Europe of the Middle Ages. Nationalism in much of Southeast Asia is a recent phenomenon, largely confined to elite groups who have been exposed to Western education and Western ways of life. For the rest, the region is a vast agglomeration of special interests, characterized more by mutual suspicion than anything else. Except for the Chinese communities, which can be found throughout the region and typically dominate trade and the entrepreneurial arts, few societies in Southeast Asia can even claim a substantial heritage of literacy, such as exists in Korea and Japan.

In Southeast Asia, as in Africa, most national boundaries

ignore ethnic boundaries. The borders of Laos, which were carved out of the Indo-Chinese peninsula to suit the convenience of French colonial administrators, leave a substantial proportion of the Lao people living in adjacent provinces of Burma and Thailand, while including sizable communities of Vietnamese in Laos. Other sizable colonies of Vietnamese live among the Khmers of Cambodia, who regard both the Vietnamese and the Thais as traditional enemies. The Burmans are a minority race in their own country, as are the Malays in Malaysia. In the Philippines, the Malay, Spanish, and American cultures have been swirled around in a kind of devil's brew without producing anything that the Filipinos themselves can agree to call a national personality. The 4,000-mile-long chain of islands constituting Indonesia has threatened more than once in recent decades to disintegrate into several island principalities.

Emerging from a variety of colonial experiences at the end of World War II, most of the nations of Southeast Asia lacked one or more of the essential prerequisites for viability. Most are still dependent, to some degree, on various forms of outside assistance to make up for these deficiencies. Only Thailand, which has preserved its independence for more than 700 years without a period of colonial rule, can claim stability as a nation. And even in Thailand, it is only recently that the government has been able to enforce its writ everywhere within its borders.

Although economic ties among the nations of Southeast Asia are beginning to appear, the important lines on an economic map charting the flow of trade and investment in the region lead far away, to Japan, Europe, and the United States. The countries of Southeast Asia for the most part sell raw materials on the world market in competition with one another: rice from Burma, Cambodia, Thailand, and Vietnam; tin and rubber from Indonesia and Malaysia; teak and mahogany from the Philippines, Burma, and Thailand. A common market on the European model will not make sense in Southeast Asia for a long time to come—although preferential arrangements, such as commodity agreements or common commodity marketing arrangements, could make sense between raw material producers and industrial buyers. But world trade characteristically expands most rapidly between industrial countries. Trade among the poor countries of Southeast Asia is now, and will remain for some time, very small compared to the region's dependence on markets elsewhere in the world.

However, despite their diverse heritages and interests, the countries of Southeast Asia have shared a common experience and are reacting to that experience in some fundamentally similar ways. Each traditional culture has been undermined and is to some extent disintegrating under the impact of multiple penetrations from other, more dynamic cultures. Most important and disruptive have been those of Western civilization. Little of Southeast Asia has been able to withstand the intrusion of Western administrators, missionaries, businessmen, and teachers. Alien institutions, such as commercial agriculture, and alien ideas of participatory government have proved too powerful to permit old ways to survive. Each nation in Southeast Asia is to some degree in transition to a new kind of society—the nature of which we do not know and cannot predict.

Rapid population growth is one characteristic of this transitional process. Such evidence as is available suggests that the region has only recently become one of densely populated communities. Professors Edwin O. Reischauer and John K. Fairbank, in their basic textbook, *East Asia: The Great Tradition* (New York: Houghton Mifflin, 1958), indicate that in 1800 only about 30 million people inhabited Southeast Asia. At that time, more than 300 million lived in China and about 50 million in Japan. However, while Japan's population has doubled since 1800, and about 750 million now live in mainland China, the population of Southeast Asia has increased eightfold, to approximately 250 million, almost half of whom live in Indonesia.

Economic growth is another characteristic of the transitional process, although only in Thailand, Malaysia, and Singapore has it even approximated population growth. Throughout most of the region, there has only been enough economic growth to feed discontent and frustration.

Among elite groups, particularly, the period of transition upon which all countries of Southeast Asia have entered is characterized by great expectations of a better life to come and bitter feelings against those responsible for exposing the weaknesses of traditional cultures. This amalgam of expectation and resentment is the distinguishing feature of reactive nationalism in all the transitional societies of Asia, Africa, and Latin America. It is difficult to exaggerate the psychological stresses afflicting those who have a foot, so to speak, in two cultures. Whether they succumb to despair, are tempted to violence, or are able to find some serenity in leading their countries forward will determine in large part how much peace and prosperity there is in the world for the rest of this century. More than anything else, it is their common experiences with alien cultures that have led elite groups in Southeast Asia to talk and think about regional cooperation.

Because the United States is the most powerful representative of that Western culture which has done more than any other to disturb the peace of tradition, we will have an influence, for good or ill, on the extent and quality of regional cooperation that finally evolves in Southeast Asia, even if, after the cessation of hostilities in Vietnam, we simply withdraw to our side of the Pacific.

THE CONTEMPORARY SETTING

Americans are not exposed to reportage of political events in Southeast Asia in anything like the degree that they are informed of such events in Europe, journalistic attention to the Vietnam war notwithstanding. Nor do official records give a good picture of new currents of opinion among leaders in the region; the manner in which nations talk to one another through the media of state documents, resolutions, and conferences is not conducive to greater popular understanding. To get a better picture of the particular and sometimes contradictory reasons why leaders in Southeast Asia are talking about regional cooperation today, it is necessary to take a closer look at a few of the more important countries. This I will do, without pretending to bring to the subjects the skills of a political analyst. My views are strictly personal, drawn from many visits to the region over the years and from many friendships built up while I was president of the World Bank.

Thailand. Even a few years ago, nobody in Bangkok took seriously the subject of regional cooperation unless he or she worked in the large enclave centered on the United Nations' Economic Commission for Asia (ECAFE). Particularly under its present, tireless, Burmese Secretary, U Nyun, ECAFE has been keeper of the faith in regional cooperation. Most of the important and promising institutional ideas for cooperation now being worked on (see

Chapter IV) were born in some ECAFE-sponsored conference. A study of the records of the conferences held since the commission was founded in 1947 would test the patience of Job, but the sheer persistence of ECAFE's often cumbersome bureaucratic activities has begun to penetrate the local political scene in Thailand.

The Thais have maintained their independence for more than 700 years, not by cooperating with their neighbors, but by fighting them or making deals when faced with superior force. The average Thai, a very proud individual, has open scorn for his Laotian and Cambodian neighbors; he has somewhat more respect for the Vietnamese and the Burmese, with both of whom he has fought in centuries past—winning and losing wars.

Although the Thais came from China many centuries ago and the present King's family is part Chinese, the only group the average Thai has traditionally feared is the resident overseas Chinese, who, 3.5 million strong, now account for nearly a fifth of the nation's population. The Thais have assimilated their Chinese immigrants through intermarriage perhaps more successfully than any other country in Southeast Asia. Nevertheless, the fact that a Chinese immigrant from Singapore or Hong Kong can, in a generation or two, rise very high in business, finance, and even government in Thailand has kept alive anti-Chinese racial nationalism that re-enforces a diplomacy of noninvolvement or nondependence.

Today, however, the Americans, as well as the Chinese, are seen as a threat to Thai independence. The Vietnam war brought to Thailand 50,000 U.S. troops, 6 big American airbases, a large naval base, and a swollen U.S. bureaucratic establishment in Bangkok. This is the largest foreign presence that has been permitted on Thai soil in modern history and represents a marked departure in Thai diplomacy. There was bound to be a reaction, and it set in with the Paris talks in the spring of 1968.

Thai politicians who were closely identified with the American build-up are understandably uneasy over the inability of the United States to bring the war in Vietnam to a smooth conclusion. An old Thai friend of mine, stopping by my office in New York recently, expressed his feelings very frankly. He told me that when the Paris talks began, he was afraid that the United States was just going to quit in Vietnam. But he was reassured by the long argument over the shape of the negotiating table, which seemed such a frustrating and pointless argument to so many Americans. "That went down well in Bangkok," my friend said. "Still," he added, "from our point of view, it seems that all the United States has succeeded in doing is to convince the North Vietnamese that they are fighting Americans and not the South Vietnamese." He left me in no doubt that he did not relish that kind of opinion growing up around the American presence in Thailand.

I am sure that my friend's views are widely held in

Bangkok and are re-enforced by the inevitable frictions that arise when substantial numbers of troops are stationed anywhere abroad. However, the U.S. presence in Thailand accomplished a great deal by way of strengthening the Thai Government. In particular, it helped the Thais to establish their authority along their very vulnerable north and northeast borders with Laos.

When I was in Bangkok four years ago, an American official told me of a survey that had been made of the north and northeast provinces. Washington was justly afraid that the Communist insurgency in Laos would spill over into these provinces and that the Thais were not then prepared to take counteraction. To help bring home the point, the local citizens in the northeast, mostly Lao tribesmen, were asked to name some of the foreign countries they had heard of. Atop almost everybody's list was "Bangkok." Little wonder. For decades, the Thai Government had regarded these provinces as Thailand's Siberia; officials were sent there only as punishment or as recognition for demonstrated incompetence. But even if, as recently as four years ago, it was possible to say that the United States was more interested in northeast Thailand than was the government in Bangkok, it is so no longer. The massive intervention on the part of the U.S. Government, whatever else can be said about it, has at least succeeded in persuading the Thai Government to establish its writ along its northern borders.

President Johnson and his chief representatives in Thailand, particularly Ambassador Graham Martin, who was in charge during the difficult years of the build-up of our forces, deserve a lot of credit for their foresight in helping to strengthen the Thai Government. You might say that what we failed to do in South Vietnam, we succeeded in doing in Thailand. However, it would be naive to expect the Thais to show public gratitude for this achievement. They are naturally much more interested now in lessening quickly their overt dependence on the United States. I think we should welcome this new view.

Regional cooperation is one of the choices now open to the Thai Government. It is not the only one. Thailand could, conceivably, strike a deal with the North Vietnamese Communists over the prostrate body of Laos in order to safeguard temporarily its northern frontiers. Or it could lapse back into dependence on the United States if the still precarious situation in the north and northeast begins to degenerate. The skill with which the United States exercises its diplomatic influence in the coming months will help determine the choice. The Thais will not take regional cooperation seriously if it appears to them to be simply a new justification for massive dependence on the United States.

Not only do many very friendly Thais want nothing so much now as for the U.S. Government to leave them alone, but below the top echelons of the Thai bureaucracy, few officials even take the idea of regional cooperation seriously as yet. A former associate of mine, writing from Bangkok, tells of a visit to the head of a key department concerned with electric power, whose views on the engineering surveys that the United States is carrying out at prospective damsites on the Mekong he wanted to get. The Thai official, a busy man, and one of the few really able, senior administrators in this division of the Thai Government, was aware of the surveys, but had never been briefed as to their purpose. Facing the sure prospect of electricity shortages in the Bangkok area, including the probability of power cuts, he simply turned up his hands and asked, "How can I possibly have time to study ideas like these which are so far in the future?" His point is a good one. Regional cooperation inevitably means greater strains on the pathetically inadequate administrative services in the governments of Southeast Asia. Haste can be made only slowly.

The real champions of regional cooperation in Thailand are King Bhumibol and Foreign Minister Thanat Khoman. Happily, such is their prestige that their support of the policy is reason enough to think that Thailand will set its course in this direction.

King Bhumibol plays a very special role in his country. One might say he manages the generation gap. He identifies with the upcoming generation and they with him— and not just because he is a jazz fan, and a good performer to boot. He has, for example, taken a keen interest in the development of the north and northeast provinces. Much of this work is managed outside the established government departments that would normally handle it, because the King wanted to see results quickly, and those in charge are mostly young men under forty—a rare thing for a society in which age still determines rank and status.

The King rarely misses an opportunity to use his prestige to promote the idea of regional cooperation. His first meeting with his fellow monarch in Laos took place on a boat in midstream on the Mekong River during a ceremony to inaugurate a power line between Laos and Thailand. He takes a keen interest in the work of the U.N. Mekong Committee, which is charged with promoting regional projects throughout the lower Mekong basin. He has given his personal support to the new Asian Institute of Technology in Bangkok (see Chapter IV). These royal acts are more than expressions of hobbies or matters of protocol. They involve the overt encouragement of younger officials, who often have traveled more and had more education than their elders. We may well see in Thailand, when the present generation of political leaders retires or dies off, not just a continuation of a very rapid rate of economic growth, which has come partly as a result of the Vietnam war, but also a gradual spread of more representative forms of government and a far more active interest in working with neighboring countries. If this happens, King Bhumibol will deserve much of the credit.

Foreign Minister Thanat Khoman has come as close as anybody in Southeast Asia to playing the role of Europe's Jean Monnet in regional affairs. He has personally mediated conflicts between the Philippines and Malaysia and helped to end the "confrontation" that President Sukarno of Indonesia attempted to impose on Malaysia in 1963. In 1961, he was a principal architect of the Association of Southeast Asia (ASA), a grouping of the Philippines, Malaysia, and Thailand. In 1967, he and Adam Malik, Foreign Minister of Indonesia, were the chief drafters of the charter of the successor organization to ASA, the Association of Southeast Asian Nations (ASEAN), which brought Indonesia and Singapore together with the three original members of ASA. Last March, Thanat Khoman announced on behalf of his government that Thailand was renouncing its long-standing border claims against Cambodia. Not only was this an important step within Thailand, where in certain regions it is still considered good politics to campaign against Cambodia, but it was also the Foreign Minister's way of saying to his colleagues in Southeast Asia that the time had come to bury some of the many hatchets lying around and start working together. Chances are that Thanat Khoman will try to see to it that, at very high levels, the work of cooperation goes on in ASEAN, which, in the wake of hostilities in Vietnam, may become the most important regional organization in Southeast Asia.

No review of the trend toward acceptance of regional

cooperation in Thailand is complete without mention of Governor Puey Ungphakorn of the Central Bank of Thailand. Governor Puey calls regular meetings of the heads of central banks in Southeast Asia to discuss financial and economic matters of common concern. Himself the leader of one of the most effective institutions of its kind in any transitional society, Governor Puey has no doubt that Thailand must in the future share its experiences widely with its neighbors in the region.

Indonesia. The preamble of the charter of ASEAN reflects, among other things, how views of regional cooperation in Indonesia differ from those in Thailand. The key portions of the preamble are as follows:

> . . . the countries of Southeast Asia share a primary responsibility for strengthening the economic and social stability of the region and ensuring their peaceful and progressive national development, and . . . they are determined to ensure their stability and security from external interference in any form or manifestation in order to preserve their national identities.
>
> . . . all foreign bases are temporary and remain only with the expressed concurrence of the countries concerned and are not intended to be used directly or indirectly to subvert the national independence and freedom of states in the area.

When he talks about regional cooperation, Indonesia's disarmingly candid Foreign Minister Adam Malik usually stresses first the need to get rid of foreign military bases. He leaves his visitor in no doubt about his intention to keep Indonesia out of any kind of entangling alliances with great powers abroad, and that includes the United States. He reminds his visitors that Indonesia has diplomatic relations with Hanoi and has offered the United Nations a peace-keeping force for Vietnam, should one be needed. He has little that is encouraging to say about such regional organizations as the Asian and Pacific Council (ASPAC), which was formed in 1966 on the initiative of the South Korean Government and includes among its members Japan, Australia, and New Zealand. In his view that kind of arrangement is too pro-Western for Indonesia.

He shows little fear of aggression from Red China and seems more concerned with the burgeoning economic penetration of the region by Japan. A friend of mine asked him what role he thought the United States should play in promoting regional cooperation in Southeast Asia. His answer could be summarized in one word: money. "You must leave the flower of regional cooperation to our initiative," he said.

Adam Malik's foreign policy is basically a reflection of Indonesia's dire internal problems. President Sukarno, when he ruled Indonesia, mobilized foreign policy in support of his desperate efforts to find solutions to his problems at home. In the 1950's, the Sukarno-inspired "spirit of Bandung" gave Indonesians a vision of Afro-Asian solidarity, but in the end this turned out to be just one more on the heaping plateful of slogans that Sukarno tried to feed his people instead of rice. His "confrontation" with Malaysia was another such slogan. He ended up, of course, hitching his country to Red China's star and bringing on his people a hideous massacre of Indonesians by Indonesians, which may have cost a quarter of a million lives.

Foreign Minister Malik and his President, General Suharto, are not going to lead Indonesia down that path again. In fact, the one important political achievement of the Suharto government has been the substitution of rice for slogans in the order of official policy priorities. However, Indonesia's foreign policy remains a reflection of its domestic troubles. When an American in Djakarta recently asked a young Indonesian diplomat if his government were serious about offering a peace-keeping force to the United Nations, the answer was typical of Indonesian pragmatism. "Certainly," the young diplomat said. "There are three reasons: first, we want to get as many generals out of the country as possible; second, we want to re-equip the army through the U.N. budget; third, we want to get smuggling out of military hands and back into civilian hands."

How Indonesia copes with its internal political problems may be as important for the future of Southeast Asia as what happens in Vietnam. It is a near miracle that General Suharto has survived since he came to power in 1965 and that Indonesia has not been subjected to an even more disastrous fate than that which attended Sukarno's downfall.

One legacy of Sukarno's rule was an inflation reminiscent of Germany just before Hitler came to power or China just before the fall of Chiang Kai-shek. Prices rose 639 per cent in 1966 alone, and another 200 per cent in 1967 and 1968. In a more developed society, this kind of inflation would certainly have led to anarchy or civil war or the imposition of the most ruthless kind of tyranny. In Indonesia, it did lead to the army's taking complete charge of the country. But General Suharto is no Hitler. One of his first acts was to invite the International Monetary Fund and the World Bank to help him out of his dire financial straits and to ask the so-called Inter-Governmental Group on Indonesia, composed of more than a dozen nations, to rescue his nation with financial aid. Inflation was abruptly halted, at least temporarily, in 1969, thanks to quick action by the IMF and the cumulative effect of the nearly $1 billion in stabilization funds that had come as a result of the Inter-Governmental Group's activities during the years 1967–69. (Washington had hoped that the United States could limit its share to one-third, with Japan providing another third, and the rest coming from Western Europe, Canada, Australia, and New Zealand. However, the U.S. share has, in fact, been significantly larger and Japan's significantly smaller.) The price of rice in the winter of 1968–69 remained stable; a year earlier, it had increased 48 per cent; over the three-year period preceding 1968, it increased tenfold. Over-all inflation in the spring of 1969 was reduced to less than 0.5 per cent a month. At least for the moment, Indonesia has responded well to the ministrations of what might be called the international financial Red Cross.

Another legacy from Sukarno, the suppression of virtually all organized civilian participation in Indonesia's political life, unfortunately is going to be harder to overcome. Although General Suharto has said he wants to return to civilian rule as soon as possible, there is no guarantee that he will be able to persuade his military colleagues of the wisdom of this course. Nor is it sure that Indonesia, despite its immensely rich resources, will become sufficiently involved in development to prevent another popular uprising. Indonesians are perhaps the least development-minded people in Southeast Asia (after the Laotians and the Cambodians, that is). The months immediately ahead will be crucial; they will determine whether Indonesia can move from stabilization to development, and from military to civilian rule, or whether the country will stagnate again until there is further upheaval.

A letter I received not long ago from Djakarta takes a rather gloomy view. It is worth recording for the light it casts on the role of the international community in Indonesian affairs today. My correspondent, an American, wrote:

> What is going on in the Indonesian Planning Ministry, BAPPANAS, strikes me as rather melancholy. Two very bright and energetic Indonesian economists, both trained at Berkeley, each enjoying the ear of General Suharto, preside over the most grandiose exercise in development planning ever attempted in Indonesia. Neither has a bilingual secretary capable of opening the mail in the morning. But they are supported by a team of ten from the World Bank (headed by an American); a team of ten from the International Monetary Fund (headed by a Turk); a team of ten American economists from the Harvard Development Advisory Services (financed by the Ford Foundation); and a smaller team of linear-programers from a Dutch economic institute.
>
> To this small army of economic advisers must be added missions from each Specialized Agency of the United Nations and from each of the major donors in the Inter-Governmental Group. The U.S. aid mission, now including 40 professionals, is, I fear, in danger of ballooning to 90 or more in the near future. By contrast, the Asian Development Bank has a modest, 3-man mission headed by a Japanese, the only Japanese on any of the international staffs. But then what the Japanese lack in representation on official missions, they make up in businessmen. There may be as many as 2,000 Japanese businessmen resident in Indonesia now. By contrast, the Germans, with 157 resident businessmen, the second largest contingent, seem very modest indeed.

What makes me melancholy about all this is that the work of the official missions appears to be so abstract. A high United Nations official characterizes the current planning exercise as "an attempt to foist a list of untested projects on a group of uncomprehending ministers." It is hard not to agree when you see how pathetically feeble the civil services are here in Djakarta. Yet this planning exercise is the great hope for a return to civilian rule. It would be tragic if the effect of all this benevolent intrusion by the international community were to relieve Indonesia's military leaders of some of their responsibility for trying to devise representative forms of government in which the diverse communities of this country can participate. . . . Even the student organization, KAMI, which played such a big role in easing out Sukarno, for which it was rewarded by General Suharto with representation in the Indonesian Parliament, has all but disbanded.

The letter concluded by saying that "the cynics here believe that the army will rule in one way or another for twenty-five years." If this proves true, it will be dangerous, for Indonesia is not like Korea, where the military regime has demonstrated that it has solid popular support. But I believe that Indonesia is too big and too diversified to be ruled forever by its army.

The sheer volume of foreign advisers in Djakarta leads me to wonder if we have not forgotten some things we should have learned from our experience elsewhere with the complexities of development finance. One crucial need in a country like Indonesia is to economize on the demands made on the scarce supply of administrative talent. Overly elaborate development planning exercises usually have the opposite result. However, a very wise Japanese counselor to General Suharto, who lives in Tokyo and travels often to Djakarta, suggests that we need not worry too much. "Indonesia," he says, "is the best advised country in the world today. Officials listen to advice very well, even to contradictory advice."

The Indonesians know theirs is the biggest country in Southeast Asia, and they do not want to be "saved" by any group of outsiders. My Japanese friend believes that they will determine their own destiny. Whether that destiny will promote or inhibit regional cooperation is very much an open question.

Malaysia. A former colleague of mine, who not long ago looked into the state of education in Indonesia and Malaysia, had interesting interviews with officials in each country. Noting that Indonesia was about to send forty-six teachers of mathematics and science to Malaysia for a year, he asked Indonesia's Minister of Education why this was being done. "The Malays," the Minister said, "have a cultural conviction that they cannot be engineers. They think only the Chinese can do that. We in Indonesia have overcome this kind of inferiority complex, so we are sending a team to help them do the same."

A day later, the Malaysian Minister of Education, when asked the same question, said, "We have to show the Indonesians how democracy works. They have never had any experience with it."

The two stories illustrate perhaps the most formidable obstacle to regional cooperation in Southeast Asia. In Malaysia—as the devastating riots of May, 1969, have shown—racial cooperation is a brute necessity. So, too, are democratic forms of government—now put aside, one hopes temporarily. Of Malaysia's nearly 10 million citizens, 36 per cent are Chinese, 45 per cent Malays, and the rest largely Tamils, of Indian origin. Indonesia, with only 3 to 4 million Chinese living among the 115 million Indonesians, is under no such constraints; as a result, the army particularly persecutes the Chinese in a hundred different ways.

When one talks about regional cooperation with a Malaysian, the subject quickly turns to Indonesia. It is not just that in 1963 Malaysia was "confronted," albeit grotesquely, by an armed threat from Sukarno. The Malaysian Government, under attack from within by fanatical, right-wing Moslem groups who advocate anti-Chinese racial policies on the Indonesian model, fears that Indonesia may encourage these groups. The Malaysian Government's concern over Indonesia was set out in an *aide-mémoire,* circulated to friendly embassies many months ago. The first paragraph of that document reads:

The events of the last decade have vividly demonstrated that the security of Malaysia and of Southeast Asia is inevitably linked to the situation in Indonesia. For as long as doubts remain regarding her intentions or stability, any revision of Malaysia's existing defense arrangements must be approached with the greatest caution and any plan for regional cooperation, which included Indonesia, can be expected to yield little in the way of fruitful or practical results.

Ever since 1963, the British have been discussing with the Malaysian Government the withdrawal of their forces from Malaysia and Singapore. The *aide-mémoire* anticipated that decision. It has now been made; the British will be gone by 1971. Nothing has happened yet to reassure those responsible for the memorandum.

Malaysia's strategic position poses a problem of great difficulty to the Western powers, especially to the United States. In the wake of Britain's announcement of its scheduled withdrawal, both Australia and New Zealand offered unilateral guarantees of military support to the Malaysians. These guarantees by our partners in the ANZUS pact mean pressure on Washington to make its position clear. Preoccupation with Vietnam naturally has made any reassessment of our strategic role in Southeast Asia impossible. But the time will come shortly when it will have to be done.

Malaysia has been largely ignored in U.S. diplomacy

during the course of the Vietnam war, despite the fact that in the 1950's Malaysia and Singapore were closer to being taken over by the Communists than has ever been the case with South Vietnam. Thanks to brilliant military tactics on the part of the British and equally brilliant political tactics on the part of Tunku Abdul Rahman, now Prime Minister of Malaysia, and Lee Kwan Yew, now Prime Minister of Singapore, the threat was put down—with, of course, nothing approaching the investment that the United States has made in Vietnam.

Since the troubles of the 1950's, Malaysia has counted on development to keep viable Southeast Asia's one multi-racial democratic nation. In no transitional society that I know of has so much been sacrificed in the name of development. Development expenditures have taken precedence over defense expenditures in the Malaysian budget to the point where there is something to show in virtually every community. But Malaysia is by no means a stable, well-integrated society, as was illustrated during the racial rioting that followed the election of May, 1969. Malays and Chinese work together in the daytime, but go home to their separate communities at night, and at the first hint of trouble, the town and city centers tend to become no-man's-lands. Until this year, the cause of democracy and racial cooperation in Malaysia was maintained precariously by a dwindling group of comrades-in-arms who were identified with Malaysian independence and the fight against the Communists. These men have been upholding the cause very largely by following sound and imaginative development policies. What will happen now to what Abdul Rahman used to call "happy Malaysia" remains to be seen.

U.S. diplomacy has not always made the tasks of Malaysia's leaders easier. On one recent occasion, Washington showed a particular lack of understanding, much to the embarrassment of our friends in Kuala Lumpur and our diplomats throughout the region. In February, 1969, the Malaysian Government let it be known that it intended to buy ten obsolescent fighter aircraft. The stated reason was the announcement of Britain's intended withdrawal in 1971, but the real reason was a squabble with another neighbor, the Philippines. The Philippine Government, apparently to indulge a tiny Moslem representation in its Parliament, has for some years now been sustaining a claim to the Malaysian state of Sabah. The Moslem leader of that part of North Borneo, where the legal title was left in a tangle of confusion by successive colonial masters, led his people into the Malaysian Federation in 1963 on the heels of a near-unanimous vote. When aircraft of the Philippine air force began buzzing Sabahan fishing boats late in 1968, he called on Kuala Lumpur for support. Sabah, in East Malaysia, is a long way from Kuala Lumpur in west Malaysia, and it seemed only prudent politics to the Malaysian Government to use the occasion to add a bit of power to its air force.

The United States became involved in this affair after routine consultations with the British in London leaked to the press in a form suggesting that the United States opposed the purchase. Soon thereafter, the State Department in Washington, referring to an amendment to the Foreign Assistance Act, directed primarily at Latin America, issued a gratuitous public statement to the effect that Congress was calling for the suspension of U.S. aid to any country that bought military equipment unnecessarily. This pronouncement thoroughly embarrassed our ambassadors in Kuala Lumpur, Bangkok, and Djakarta, for the Malaysian Government had taken the trouble to check its intentions in advance with both Indonesia and Thailand, neither of which objected. I do not mean to suggest that the United States should take sides in squabbles like that between Malaysia and the Philippines, but it does seem that in this case we could have shown the diplomatic good sense to say nothing. We will have to do much better if we are to be serious about promoting regional cooperation.

Of all the countries in Southeast Asia, Malaysia and Singapore have the most to gain from regional cooperation, and the most to lose from any precipitate withdrawal by the United States from the region. It is not a question of economic assistance; Malaysia is not asking for that from the United States; there has never been a U.S. aid mission in Kuala Lumpur. What is needed is some understanding for the "good boys" of Southeast Asia—some recognition of their achievements and of their remaining, exceedingly difficult problems.

Singapore. Prime Minister Lee Kwan Yew of Singapore and Prime Minister Tunku Abdul Rahman of Malaysia worked hand in hand in the 1950's when the Communists threatened to take over the whole peninsula. But cooperation against the Communists did not lead to enduring cooperation between the largely Chinese city of Singapore and the predominantly Malay state of Malaysia. Prime Minister Lee broke up a fledgling federation of Malaysia and Singapore, which the British had designed, because he feared his Chinese city-state was not ready to participate in a government in which Malays would inevitably hold most of the high posts and that would be threatened by fanatical, right-wing Malay groups. Like so much of the brief history of regionalism in Southeast Asia, the federation idea was politically premature, however logical it was from an economic point of view.

Still, Lee Kwan Yew knows that Singapore's future safety and prosperity depend on regional cooperation within Asia. "I would like to see an Asia," he said recently, "particularly my immediate part of Asia, largely self-sustaining, interlocked . . . in trade, commerce, and industrialization programs, economic growth and mutual security with a minimum of direct support of intervention from the outside." But, as one of his chief lieutenants put it to me recently, "We have so much to gain that we cannot get out in front."

In 1966, Lee floated a trial balloon while on a visit to New Delhi, hoping to persuade the Indonesian Government to join him in a proposal for all-Asian regional cooperation. He was ignored. Singapore is one of the five founding members of ASEAN, but given the hostility of Malaysia and Indonesia, Prime Minister Lee has little leverage and little opportunity to play a constructive role. I suspect he is glad that ASEAN has been formed, if only for the participation of Thailand and the Philippines, which tends to diminish somewhat the influence of the other two members.

Lee's best defense of his island home has been his remarkable record of pulling Singapore up by its own bootstraps. Of Singapore's 2 million people, 75 per cent are Chinese; Indians and Malays, in approximately equal portions, make up most of the rest. Lee rules them all with an energy and imagination that puts me in mind of Fiorello LaGuardia when he was Mayor of New York City.

Three out of every four Singaporeans are under thirty-five years of age, and the Singapore Government is the youngest and the most exciting in Southeast Asia. Every important official talks as though he were head of the local Chamber of Commerce. The city's social services are the best in Southeast Asia, if not in all of Asia, Africa, and Latin America. American city planners, in fact, could well afford to visit Singapore—not to teach but to learn. Officials claim one new apartment unit is completed every thirty-eight minutes. Every child goes to school, even though it is necessary to teach four separate languages—Malay, Tamil, Chinese, and English.

One of Singapore's most notable successes has been in family planning. There are twenty-eight so-called all-times family planning clinics listed in the Singapore telephone book. I am told that they are not all open round the clock as the phrase "all times" suggests, but they are an indication of the fantastic success that the Singapore Government has had in controlling population growth. Between 1959 and 1967, population rose at the threatening rate of over 3 per cent a year. In 1969, the rate will be below 2 per cent. I doubt that any other city of this size in the world can show such a dramatic change in such a short time.

Most important, everybody in Singapore is working as hard as he can to catch up with Hong Kong and Taiwan, Singapore's major competitors for trade and industry. The figures are impressive: manufacturing output has grown almost 25 per cent each year for the past three years; exports of manufactures have increased 250 per cent since 1960. But there is still a long way to go. The British withdrawal from the Singapore naval base threatens thousands of jobs in the city. And out of a work force of some 600,000, perhaps 50,000, mostly young people with high school training, are unemployed.

Prime Minister Lee likes to tell visitors how he has reversed an old adage about the climate. "The North Chinese," he says, "look down on the South Chinese, and the South Chinese look down on the Thais. The Thais look down on the Malays, who thought they could look down on us. But then we got air-conditioning." Singaporeans can justly boast that they know how to develop in a hot climate.

With the British pulling out their defense forces, Singapore, as much as Malaysia, is anxiously watching the United States to see what we are going to do. Lee has stoutly supported us in Vietnam, always "assuming," as he put it, "that you are serious." But in November, 1968, he took an extended vacation in the United States, much of which he spent talking with the faculty and students at Harvard University, and he returned to Singapore badly shaken by what he termed the "irresolution" of Americans over their future role in Asia. With Singapore squeezed as it is between a hostile Malaysia and a hostile Indonesia, Lee probably could not radically alter his foreign policy even were he so inclined. But if the United States indeed turns out to be as irresolute as the Prime Minister thought after his visit, he or a successor could become another neutralist Prince Sihanouk, simply in order to survive.

Such a shift would be costly in terms of U.S. interests. Singapore is one of the key centers for the 12-to-14 million overseas Chinese who live in Southeast Asia. Among the Chinese communities in the region, there is already an extensive network of regional cooperation, based on Chinese domination of much of the region's trade and finance. The Chinese Communists and the Republic of China on Taiwan continue to wrestle for the allegiance of these communities, thereby posing ticklish diplomatic problems for the United States. Until the mid–1950's, it was our policy to support allegiance to the Republic of China among these peoples, but then our policy shifted to one of supporting their assimilation in their host countries. Ironically, Peking made a similar shift in policy in 1958, concluding a treaty with President Sukarno that promised assimilation of Indonesia's Chinese. In 1959–60, even the Republic of China shifted to a policy of encouraging assimilation.

However, one is tempted to agree with those who say, "Once a Chinese, always a Chinese." Assimilation at best is a long-range hope. Peking broke diplomatic relations with Djakarta after the aborted coup of 1965; the Red Chinese have maintained a drumfire of opposition to the government in Thailand and may well adopt a similar attitude in Malaysia. All this could mean trouble for Prime Minister Lee. Lee remains the only major leader in Southeast Asia who has cowed his Communist opponents and given the overseas Chinese an image of something better than either assimilation or oppression. A thriving Singapore, together with Hong Kong and Taiwan, encourages thoughts of an alternative to Communism in China. Regional cooperation is the best hope, I think, for keeping that alternative alive. What would kill it very quickly would be a precipitate withdrawal of the United States from the region.

The Philippines. An acquaintance of mine flew into Manila recently with a young Filipino professor from the city of Zamboanga on the island of Mindanao. Remembering that this is a Moslem community, situated just opposite the Malaysian state of Sabah, my acquaintance asked his traveling companion what he thought about the argument which the Philippine and Malaysian governments were having over the status of Sabah. "Oh, it has benefited us," the young Filipino said. "Smuggling is the big business in Zamboanga. Both our government and the Malaysians used to operate customs patrols in the waters between Sabah and Zamboanga. The patrols were not very effective, but they were some hindrance. Now they are gone and traffic flows more freely."

I keep hearing stories like this about the Philippines, and they always depress me. A front-page scandal of February, 1969, I understand, involved higher education; it appears that diploma mills have become one of the country's half-dozen most profitable businesses. Or so at least said a report of a committee of the Philippine Senate, the members of which were no doubt very interested in their country's presidential election campaign.

Yet last year, in the Philippines, there occurred one of the most remarkable economic breakthroughs in modern time. Thanks to the new "miracle" seeds developed at the Los Banõs Agricultural Research Station not far from Manila, the country produced enough rice for the first time in half a century to feed its rapidly expanding population (the rate of growth is about 3.5 per cent a year) without having to resort to imports. It happened almost overnight when the Filipinos finally found an organization within their own government capable of getting seeds and fertilizers to masses of cultivators.

I would like to think that this kind of economic breakthrough would have its reflection in Philippine politics, but friends who write me from Manila are not encouraging. People in Manila, even more than in Bangkok and Djakarta, tend to regard the hinterland of their country as beyond the pale. When elections come along, voters in the cities vote one way and voters in the countryside another. It seems part of the Southeast Asian way of life that the capital city should always vote against the government. Manila, particularly, reflects deep pessimism and a marked discontent with its government. Dissatisfaction with the steady deterioration of public and civil services is more keenly felt than ever, even among those banking friends of mine who usually judiciously avoid any comments on Philippine politics.

Whether the future brings to Manila political reform,

revolution, or just more of the same incapacity to govern, relations with the United States are bound to be in the thick of things. Even talk of regional cooperation leads inevitably to the question of the Filipino's ambivalent attitudes toward the United States. In fact, the major reason why the subject is discussed at all is a vague feeling among many Philippine leaders that their country should establish an Asian "identity" in order to assert its independence from the United States. But although it is standard fare in Philippine politics to lambaste the United States from time to time over the presence of military bases or over the special privileges still accorded to U.S. businessmen under Philippine law, the Philippine Government has not had much success establishing a good image with its Asian neighbors. And Philippine diplomacy in Southeast Asia has so far stopped short of any move that might seem to lessen the country's ties with the United States. There may be a lot of anti-American rhetoric in Philippine politics, but there is yet little inclination to take anti-American positions.

In the immediate future, U.S. diplomacy will have more effect in the Philippines than in any other Southeast Asian nation. And the place that the promotion of regional cooperation has in our diplomacy will be more important in our relations with the Philippines than with any other country. We have to ask ourselves if it is not, perhaps, in our interests as well as theirs that the Filipinos actively cultivate more of an Asian identity so that their government can play a more constructive role in regional cooperation.

The American Argument

All things considered, it would be easy to write off the idea of regional cooperation in Southeast Asia as absurd. Age-old mutual suspicions still dominate politics and diplomacy. No enduring competitor to the extended family system has yet appeared to mitigate the intolerance and the corruption which, in our eyes, that traditional system contains within it. The political outlook, even in Thailand, Malaysia, and Singapore, where the subject of regional cooperation is taken most seriously, is clouded by upheaval and threats of upheaval. Indonesia and the Philippines must at present be considered more as obstacles to than agents of regional cooperation, official pronouncements to the contrary.

It is well to face honestly these realities, for any U.S. policy in Southeast Asia in the immediate future must recognize that in all probability there will be a great deal of turmoil in this part of the world in the years immediately ahead. But these are not enduring realities. It is possible to argue that regional cooperation has to come if, in the long run, the nations of Southeast Asia are to maintain their identities and avoid the kind of anarchy that will invite Chinese domination. For those Chinese who live in the region, regional cooperation keeps alive the hope for a more tolerant day in China itself as well as for that kind of acceptance which will permit the enormous energies and talents of these communities to be used constructively for the benefit of all.

Of course, from an Asian's point of view, nothing in the future is inevitable except the continued impact of the past. So I am making the kind of argument that only a Westerner can make. And I am making it from the point of view of the United States's real national interests—saying that it is very important to stress this kind of inevitability and help in every way we can to hasten acceptance of it.

Before exploring how we can, however, I must turn to Japan. Japan is again a major power in Southeast Asia. As far as the United States is concerned, Japan is the most important country in Asia today, for what Japan is willing to do will determine in large part what the United States can and should be prepared to do itself.

III

"Japan Ought..."

THE EMBASSY of Japan in Djakarta, Indonesia, makes an interesting contrast to the American Embassy. Ours is a complex of two- and three-story structures in a nondescript neocolonial style, one of which houses Embassy staff, another the personnel of the Agency for International Development. The Japanese Embassy looks like a modern apartment house of eight or nine stories, with a low, two-story wing on one side. The wing houses a very small Japanese diplomatic mission; the high-rise section is occupied entirely by Japanese businessmen.

The U.S. presence in Indonesia reflects our government's interpretation of its world-wide, strategic responsibilities. The Japanese are in Indonesia to buy and sell things. When the budget of the Japanese Foreign Office proved insufficient to complete their Embassy building, businessmen made up the deficit.

The "Indonesia boom" is the talk of business circles

in Tokyo. Within the next year or two, Japan is very likely to displace the United States as the largest foreign investor in Indonesia, moving up from fifth place last year. Unlike American investments, which are concentrated in oil, sulphur, and nickel, Japanese investments will be diffused widely throughout the economy and the geography of the country.

The increase in Japan's trade with Southeast Asian nations in the 1960's has been spectacular. Although Indonesia exported less altogether in 1967 than in 1960, its exports to Japan increased fivefold in those years. Thailand's exports to Japan doubled in the same period and its imports from Japan tripled. Despite the Vietnam war, Thailand spends one third of its foreign exchange trade acccount in Japan, as against only 17 per cent in the United States. The Philippines still buy a bit more in the United States than in Japan, but Japanese exports account for about one-third of Philippine imports today as against about one-fifth in 1960. Between 1965 and 1968, Japanese exports to Malaysia increased by one-third, while exports to Singapore increased by 50 per cent.

The U.S. Government estimates that in 1968 Japan earned about $1 billion on its balance of payments as a result of the Vietnam war and related activities. Japanese exports to South Vietnam alone have increased from $30 million to $190 million over the past four years. The Japanese are eager to sell in both North and South Vietnam. The huge Mitsui Trading Company has even estab-

lished within its organization an "Indochina Reconstruction Committee" in anticipation of participating in the
postwar reconstruction of both halves of Vietnam.

American officials, looking beyond the end of hostilities
in Vietnam, envisage a big role for Japan in the affairs of
Southeast Asia. Well they might. Japan's post-World War
II recovery and boom has carried the country to third place
among the world's economic powers, surpassing even the
hard-working Germans. Only the United States and the
Soviet Union have greater national wealth. Japan's gross
national product has been increasing at the phenomenal
rate of about 10 per cent annually throughout the 1960's,
but the country still spends less than 1 per cent of the
total on its own defense. It is not surprising that policy
planners in Washington begin many of their papers and
discussions with the phrase "Japan ought . . ."

Japan ought, they say, to be willing to match its tremendous economic achievements with a political view of
its role in the world that would relieve the United States
of some of its responsibilities in East Asia. Japan ought
to be the kind of partner of the United States in East
Asian affairs that Germany and Britain have been in
European affairs. Japan ought to devote a greater share of
its wealth to providing economic assistance to Southeast
Asia over and above the convenience of its traders and
investors. And Japan ought—within the confines of its
"pacifist" constitution—to begin to face up to its own
defense needs and not rely so completely on the shield

provided by the armed forces of the United States under the successive security treaties between the two nations.

Understandable as these reactions are, it is dangerously romantic to conclude that what we think Japan ought to do will correspond exactly to Japan's own view of its national interests. It is dangerous also to assume that the nations of Southeast Asia think the way we do about Japan's future role. The Japanese view of the world today bears some resemblance to our view of the world in the 1920's, when Calvin Coolidge was saying that "the business of America is business" and dismissing the problems of hard-pressed European debtors with the observation that "They hired the money, didn't they?" In Southeast Asia, memories of ill-treatment under Japan's "Greater East Asia Co-Prosperity Sphere" and resentment against the tactics Japanese traders and investors employ in their current trade and investment drive make leaders suspicious of a future in which the United States encourages Japan to take the primary role in development of the area.

Since our relations with Japan are likely to be the most important of any in our foreign policy in the years immediately before us (those with Russia possibly excepted), it is well to explore the prospects honestly and hardheadedly.

THE U.S. IMPACT ON JAPAN

The impact that the United States has had on Japan over the past hundred years is a fascinating story. It is one that few Americans know, perhaps because, except for World War II, Japanese affairs have had relatively little impact on the United States. One man who has done much to reconstruct this story through the painstaking process of translating books and documents is Edward Seidensticker of the University of Michigan, who has resided in Japan off and on for many years and was honored by being asked to be the official interpreter for the Japanese author and poet, Kawabata Yasunari, on his journey to Oslo, Norway, to receive the Nobel Prize for literature in 1968.

Professor Seidensticker began an essay a few years ago with a delightful story, drawn from the early years of the Meiji restoration in Japan, which illustrates the nature of America's earliest impact on Japan:

> The Empress of Japan has just been the recipient of an edifying lecture. The lecturer has been her husband's tutor in Confucianism, and the subject has been a series of wise sayings by a wise man from the West. To demonstrate that she has learned her lesson well, the Empress indites a series of thirty, one-syllable poems in elegant, lady-like Japanese; and, to cap his own argument, the tutor composes a poem in masculine Chinese. The Empress's first poem is a gentle little flourish about how her loyal subjects are expected to behave when the cherries are in bloom or the maple leaves aflame, and the tutor's first quatrain is a crisper sally having to do with a flower beloved of the Chinese, the plum.
> And who is their foreign model, and what did he say? It

is Benjamin Franklin. "Eat not to dullness, drink not to elevation," he said.

Both tutor and Empress, Seidensticker went on to explain, were in harmony with the spirit of their day.

> The wisdom of the West was seen not as a challenge to tradition but as a means of preserving it. . . . Indeed, foreign learning was hardly thought of as wisdom at all, but rather as a mass of techniques. Japan was the repository of wisdom, and the techniques were but to shore it up. Franklin had had some ideas that had obviously worked. So why not make use of them? *

From the Meiji period to the present, Japan's modernization has involved the adaptation of a mass of techniques from the West. But those who thereby conclude that the Japanese are "mere copiers" have missed the point entirely. The Japanese do not consider it humiliating to be a good pupil from time to time in their relations with other nations, particularly with the United States. Although they may have some ambiguous feelings about their cultural relationship with the Chinese, the Japanese have never felt that any other culture was wiser than theirs. Japan is unique in that it was able to move from a traditional to a modern society while keeping more or less intact its fundamental traditions.

---

* Edward Seidensticker, *The United States and Japan* (Englewood Cliffs, N.J.: Prentice-Hall, 1966), pp. 5–6.

The fifty years before the turn of the century were the halcyon days when America was teacher and Japan was pupil. The most surprising things were exported from America to Japan in those years. A founder of one of Japan's first Socialist parties was converted to Socialism, according to Seidensticker, at the Hartford (Connecticut) Theological Seminary. At least some of those who launched the first labor unions in Japan were inspired to do so after a visit to San Francisco. An American teacher in a Japanese agricultural school left in his farewell address a phrase in English known to every Japanese schoolboy today: "Be ambitious, boys!"

After the turn of the century, the relationship began to change. The Japanese bitterly resented the discriminatory laws passed by the state of California, which, on the one hand, encouraged the importation of cheap Japanese labor and, on the other, forced the immigrants into segregated schools and barred marriage to other than Japanese. Simultaneously, sympathies in America shifted from the by now strong government of Japan to the weak government of China. The Japanese, for their part, gradually ceased to regard themselves as pupils and by the time of Pearl Harbor were acting like ruthless masters.

There are those who see some repetition of this cycle in American-Japanese relations in the post-World War II period. Indeed, Japanese even today like to warn their American friends that Japan is always a "good boy" when it is acting as pupil, but that this behavior is not likely to last. However, Seidensticker rejects this neat view of the matter, and I agree with him. Since World War II, our relationships have grown much more complicated because they have become more intimate at the same time they have become more realistic. Americans and Japanese who know each other are beginning to take their separate peculiarities more for granted. The question is whether enough of us know enough about each other to weather some very stormy years immediately ahead.

On one point everyone is in agreement: the Japanese today, for the first time in twenty-three years, are beginning to think seriously about what their role in the world should be. They are starting with the assumption that their relationship with the United States, which they have come to regard as subservient, must change. The concrete issues, of course, are the future status of Okinawa, with its 900,-000 Japanese and its key American air and naval bases, and the future of the Treaty of Mutual Cooperation and Security, which, when it was fashioned in 1960, caused sufficient rioting in Tokyo to force President Eisenhower to cancel a proposed visit. The Treaty reaches a milestone in 1970: it can be extended simply by dint of both sides taking no action; it can be formally renewed; or it can be scrapped.

It is important that Americans who are concerned with our future policies in East Asia try to understand the state of Japanese opinion today. My own appraisal is based not on extensive residence in Japan but on some precious friendships built up over the years. I am particularly indebted to a Japanese friend for permitting me to quote brief passages from a private paper, prepared in the winter of 1968–69, in which he set forth his views of the state of official and public opinion in Japan.

THE PRESENT

One of the best indications of the hold of tradition in Japan is the role of age. By and large, age still determines both rank and salary in government and business. To be sure, there is a new generation in revolt. Over the past several months, some seventy Japanese universities have been disrupted or shut down entirely by highly regimented groups of students. These activities are as shocking to the Japanese "Establishment" as the more anarchical student groups in the United States are to our older generation. But the Establishment in Japan is much more rigid in conception than its American counterpart. And in Japan, the generation gap means something different: it is less one between generations than one between successive waves of leaders who come to positions of power rather predictably as a result of their age.

In Japan, the Establishment today is led by those who were aged thirty-five to fifty at the time of the World War II defeat, the dazed survivors of a catastrophe that had swept away the more senior leadership group. A policy of close cooperation between the United States and Japan was born when this group and the American occupation forces were "driven into each other's arms . . . bewildered by the Herculean task of administering a nation of 80 million souls," as my friend put it. The embrace has lasted a long time and has resulted in an alliance that has produced great benefits for both sides. But the very longevity of this alliance is now drawing public attention in Japan to its genesis under the occupation. The whole American security presence is being brought under scrutiny.

Total defeat at the hands of the Americans in 1945 had a profound effect on the Japanese. It shattered the ideals built up over the eight decades following the Meiji restoration and buried in the rubble any lingering notions of a militarist role for Japan in the world—a role that had commanded great national sacrifice when necessary. At the same time, the defeat, followed by a prolonged occupation, thoroughly isolated the Japanese people from any participation in the making of foreign policy. Japanese diplomacy until this day has been bereft of popular support and understanding. Now, things are changing. The Japanese are again beginning to think about their place in the world. Naturally, the readjustment process is generating complex cross-currents of feeling and mood, especially toward the United States and the long embrace between the Japanese Government and the American Government.

The process of readjustment coincides with the coming of a generational change in Japanese leadership. What the Japanese call "the wartime generation"—those who were twenty to thirty-five years of age at the time of the defeat— are beginning to take over. These men saw active military service and, in the words of my Japanese friend, "came home from the war numbed in body and spirit and suffered in silence through the evil postwar years while laboring as the workhorses of Japanese recovery and development." Of this new generation of leaders, my Japanese friend says: "They are capable, efficient, hardworking, but com-plex-ridden, ambivalent, indecisive, submissive to and simultaneously resentful of the previous generation—and, by inference, of the Americans." They will be followed by what the Japanese call the "first postwar generation," those aged twenty or younger at the time of the defeat, who my friend says are "equally capable, but relatively more rational and complex-free."

Five years from now, Japan's wartime generation will have completely taken over from the old pro-Americans. Ten years from now, they will be started on their way out. In the meantime, they will have to devise a new relationship with the United States to replace one which, in Japanese eyes, lacked the element of free choice in its origins. They recognize the basic merit of the American alliance at the same time that they resent it as an instrument of foreign pressure and subordination. They will have to define

Japan's new role in the world, while accepting greater public participation in the decision. This is the generation that will take the first halting steps toward a re-examination of Japan's security role, including discussion of nuclear weapons—hitherto the number one taboo.

The last great ordeal of the old leadership will be the defense of the U.S.–Japan security treaty in 1970. Our Japanese friends are warning us to expect a supreme effort, similar to that of 1960, from political opponents and violent groups of "irrational" activists determined to over-turn the cooperation policy. In this matter, Japan's mass media will play a crucial part.

Here again it is important to make a distinction between Japan and America. The Japanese press and television are not representatives of "the fourth estate" as we know the free press in Western countries. The press in Japan traces its origins to particular clans and families. It is by tradition antigovernment.

Under the occupation, the mass media in Japan grew to be one of the most important influences in the country, encouraged, unwittingly perhaps, by the American authori-ties. To its established antigovernment bias, the Japanese press added new biases by inclination. It borrowed some of the most extreme features of American press sensa-tionalism, but it is not favorably disposed toward the United States. It is critical of close cooperation, although not fundamentally opposed to it. The press and other media do not have a coherent or party line against U.S. policy, but they do reject subservience to America and express their resentment in certain common ways. They stress that American bases in Japan are sources of public nuisance and are not essential to Japan's defense, but only to self-serving American purposes outside Japan. The non-recognition of China by Japan is depicted a symbol of Japanese servility and Okinawa as a symbol of American occupation twenty-three years after the defeat. Even economic negotiations between the Japanese and the United States are presented in terms of evil U.S. intentions.

There is a heavy left-wing concentration in the mass media in Japan—indeed in all Japanese intellectual activities. But most Japanese with whom I have talked think this less important than the basic differences in outlook between the successive generations that are coming to power. Both the present government and the generation of leaders to follow are likely to be on the defensive among their own people. The subject of foreign policy is a confusing one to the people of Japan. From the media and elsewhere, they receive vague and sinister impressions about Japan's relationship with America, punctuated by the inevitable incidents that occur when foreign military bases are embedded in densely populated urban areas.

My friend sums up his appraisal of Japanese public opinion this way:

The Japanese people, for all their native good sense, and passive support of the cooperation policy (deriving in part from their good disposition toward America) . . . are slowly experiencing a generation change. . . . Only partially freed from their defeat-induced pacifism and phobia of nuclear weapons, they lack any real sense of external threat to their isolated island home and feel only a formless anxiety on the state of the world. . . . They cannot express themselves except by a growing distaste of what they increasingly feel to be unnecessary Japanese subservience to America, and a mounting rejection of closer military ties with the United States. . . . In the midst of an unprecedented prosperity, due mainly to the incomparably profitable relationship with the United States, they are somehow dissatisfied with their place in the world, especially *vis-à-vis* America. They feel, albeit vaguely, that the outcome of 1970 will set the tone for the coming decade.

THE FUTURE

My Japanese friend, like a good diplomat, is stating his view with a purpose. The immediate purpose is the future status of Okinawa. "The rational course for the United States," he writes, "is to return the administration and the responsibility for keeping internal order (in Okinawa) to the Japanese, and to concentrate on the maintenance of the role of the bases, thus ensuring the continuity of the alliance with Japan." His recommendation appears a sound one to me, but this subject lies outside the scope of this book, and in any case, by the time these words appear, the Okinawa issue will have proceeded a long way toward, one hopes, a mutually acceptable solution.

However, the attitudes described in my friend's paper transcend the problem of Okinawa and even the problem of the future of the U.S.–Japan security treaty. The author is at pains to say that, if Okinawa and "1970" are mishandled, whether by Japan or the United States or both, the consequences could be disastrous in terms of political developments inside Japan. I have no reason to doubt this or to think that cool heads will not prevail in these matters, on both sides of the Pacific, but even in the best of circumstances, the transfer of power from one generation of leaders to another in Japan promises several years of difficult relations before the kind of partnership of equals that U.S. policy-makers are seeking, and must seek, can become a reality.

In forecasting the future of Japanese-American relations, our friends in Japan are warning us that, in government circles, pro-Americanism, as a legacy of the generation about to leave office, is bound to dwindle rapidly for the simple reason that it was not rooted in any real appreciation of Western values, but, rather, was limited to an admiration of American strength. The old leadership was composed essentially of men of the Japanese past who temporarily transferred their allegiance to a greater power than that of the defunct Meiji state. Their successors, we are warned, are bound to try to rectify what they believe to be the more subservient aspects of Japan's relations with the United States. At the same time, we are told to expect the new generation of leaders to be generally indecisive and unlikely initiators of new activities or policies. Without strong public support, they are likely to rest on a passive lack of cooperation with the United States, just at a time when circumstances alone suggest a period of strain between our two countries.

This period of strain and indecision may last until the middle of the 1970's, when the first postwar generation begins to take power in Japan. By then, our Japanese friends say, if all has gone well, the Japanese may feel enough of a sense of equality to rejuvenate the close American relationship. By then, a sense of national dignity, combined with a massive economic potential for contributing to human welfare, may permit Japan to take the kind of position in Asia and the world that American policy-makers envision for her in a much shorter time.

To me, this view of the future does not suggest the imminence of violent revolution, or even of an abrupt change in Japanese foreign policy. Japanese society is uniquely conservative in many respects. But we should listen carefully to what our friends in Japan are saying and adjust our diplomacy accordingly. There is grave danger in judging Japanese-American relations in terms of what we think Japan ought to do and not in terms of the realities of Japanese political life and of Japan's interests as the Japanese see them.

JAPAN AND SOUTHEAST ASIA

No group follows with more attention and anxiety Japan's struggle to define for itself a new role in the world than the leaders of Southeast Asia. All quite naturally expect that as Japan's trade and investments in the region multiply, a political policy will inevitably follow. Here the suspicions rampant in the region come into play. Memories of ill-treatment during Japan's occupation of the region in World War II have much to do with these suspicions, especially in the Philippines and Indonesia. But perhaps more important today are the working habits of the Japanese trader and investor himself.

An Indonesian official tells his American visitor of being chased down the hall of his own ministry by a covey of Japanese offering 5 per cent to him personally on some deal. A Thai official complains that a Japanese investor will borrow his capital from a Thai bank, import his machinery through a Japanese importer, resident in Bangkok, and pay off the Thai bank out of his local profits, "so all that the investment means to us is a piece of machinery, which we could have imported ourselves." Indonesia passes laws demanding that foreign traders use Indonesian import-export firms. Officials explain the laws to the Japanese as a method of controlling local Chinese traders, but the explanation given to an American visitor is that the Japanese must be made to help Indonesia build up its own trading class.

"We have our problems with our swindlers," admits a young Japanese diplomat. The board chairman of Tokyo's powerful Fuji Bank told an audience of Indonesian businessmen recently, "We Japanese businessmen must admit that in the past we could not completely exclude some 'ugly Japanese' from our commercial transactions with Indonesia. We deeply regret that this has happened, and now we are strongly determined to abide by the spirit of clean business on both sides, in trade, investment, and all business relations."

The Japanese, of course, have no monopoly on corruption in Southeast Asia. Societies that still rest substantially on extended family relationships tend to follow what we in the West regard as corrupt practices. From their viewpoint, it is not necessarily corruption but family loyalty that dictates the taking of bribes or the falsification of records. More important, I think, is the fact that Japanese trading practices grow out of a business system very different from that prevailing in the West. Japanese commercial representatives abroad are, typically, representatives of Japanese trading companies, like the huge Mitsui company, which control the sale and distribution of goods both in Japan and outside. The manufacturer in Japan plays a minor role compared to his American counterpart. He does not produce at a profit the way ours do; he may even be allowed for quite some time to produce at a loss. He lives on loans from the banks and on a small measure of equity from the trading companies, who take and dispose of all of his output. Inside Japan, competition—blood-thirsty competition, in fact—exists within carefully pre-scribed limits. But abroad the Japanese salesman acts more as the representative of a state trading company than as a representative of a private enterprise, Western style.

Every Japanese salesman, at home and abroad, is as-signed a quota. Abroad the quota is fixed by the trading company and approved by the Japanese Department of Commerce, commonly called MITI. To fail to fulfill an assigned quota is not just a matter of money to a Japanese exporter; it is a matter of honor. He is on assignment not only for his company but also for MITI. He has a duty, an obligation, more important than the rights and wrongs of the matter. He will, if at all possible, avoid permitting any local importer to get between him and his customer and risk making it impossible to fulfill his obligation. In return for fulfilling his obligation, he has what amounts to life tenure with his company. It is still practically un-heard of for a Japanese "salaried" employee to quit his job with one company in favor of a job with another. He is a "company man" in a sense that makes allegiances in Amer-ican corporations seem almost frivolous. Tell a Japanese that, quite aside from corruption, Japanese business practices sometimes raise ethical and political questions in the minds of others, particularly in the minds of Westerners, and chances are he will return a blank, uncomprehending stare. After all, have we not been congratulating Japan on its phenomenal rate of growth at home and in exports abroad in recent years? By any measure of efficiency, the system does work phenomenally well.

JAPANESE FOREIGN AID

The Japanese have shown a growing interest in giving financial aid to the nations of Southeast Asia. In 1967, total Japanese official aid to the region amounted to $190 million, or about half of all official Japanese aid in that year. (Another $26 million represented private investment and export credits.) These figures will go up sharply in the years ahead. Japan has matched our $200 million contribution to the capitalization of the Asian Development Bank in Manila, to which thirty-two governments in all, including all the major Western European nations, save France, have contributed just short of $1 billion. Japan has pledged a second $100 million to the Asian Bank in the form of special grant funds for agricultural development. (As this is written, they are ahead of us in this matter; Congress has yet to approve an equal American pledge to the Asian Bank's special funds.) The Japanese Government is providing about a quarter of the present emergency assistance to Indonesia. And the Japanese have indicated a willingness to participate in a financial scheme for the reconstruction of Vietnam, one which they expect to benefit both North and South Vietnam.

In Tokyo, however, there is a running argument between the Foreign Office and the Ministry of Finance over the amount and the purposes of foreign aid that bears some resemblance to the running battle between the Congress and the Agency for International Development in Washington. The Ministry of Finance in Japan, like our Congress, is something less than enthusiastic about foreign aid. The Finance Ministry, perhaps the single most powerful unit in the Japanese Government, agrees in principle that Japan should allocate 1 per cent of its gross national product to foreign aid (it allocates only a little more than 0.5 per cent now). But the Ministry is also closer to Japanese politics than is the Foreign Office. The Japanese economy may be the second largest in the non-Communist world today, but to Japanese politicians, what counts is that per capita income in Japan is still only $921, or just behind that of Italy and just ahead of that of Ireland. Nineteen countries in all have higher per capita incomes than the Japanese. The most that the Japanese are willing to say officially now is that their foreign aid will increase "substantially" by 1980, when the gross national product may be about $500 billion against $140 billion now.

More to the point, perhaps, is the fact that the Japanese Diet at this time views foreign aid only in commercial terms. "Altruistic arguments don't work with us," says a high Japanese official. "Maybe the former colonial powers ought to feel a sense of obligation, but we were defeated in war and paid our debt in reparations." Even more to the point, perhaps, there can be no political rationale for foreign aid in Japan until the Japanese go through the agony of defining for themselves a new political role in the world.

Foreign Minister Kiichi Aichi, in an interview with *The New York Times,* said recently, "We must make a peaceful contribution to the stability of Asia by contributing as much of our economic power as we possibly can," but he repeated the frequent warning of Japanese diplomats that, because of a constitutional prohibition against building up a potential for making war, Japan will not be willing to participate in any regional defense grouping. The Foreign Office has been even more explicit. In an official briefing paper prepared at the time of President Richard M. Nixon's inaugural, the Japanese Foreign Office urged that the United States avoid placing excessive hopes on the growth of East Asian regionalism and expressed the hope that the United States would not become frustrated at the lack of Japanese cooperation or participation in promoting regionalism. Such participation was deemed just not feasible in the next decade.

Realistically, we have to accept the fact that at present there is very little prospect that Japan will be willing to become a political, much less a military, partner of the United States in Southeast Asia. What is possible, in my view, is to persuade the Japanese that between regionalism and regional cooperation there is an important difference. Making this distinction clear and persuasive to the Japanese is going to be a delicate business, for the real danger in Japanese-American relations is that we will, wittingly or unwittingly, force the Japanese to choose rearmament rather than cooperation in the years ahead. We run a grave risk of doing just this if the questions of Okinawa and the Treaty of Mutual Cooperation and Security are not considered within the context of a broad, new U.S. diplomatic policy in East and Southeast Asia.

IV

Some Steps Toward Cooperation

IF WE cannot count on Japan to be our military and political partner in Southeast Asia, if regional cooperation there faces formidable historical, cultural, and economic obstacles, what kind of cooperation can we hope to promote? In the following chapters, I will suggest some possible answers to this question.

I take it for granted that the reader realizes that regional cooperation is not a problem that can be solved. Rather, it is a promising political and diplomatic objective on which the United States can hang much of its policy in the region in the years immediately ahead. When it comes to promoting regional cooperation, the art to be cultivated is diplomacy, for it is the actions of others, not our own, that will determine whether this is a practical and useful objective.

The major continuing means open to us to influence the course of regional cooperation is, I think, development assistance. Exercising diplomacy effectively through such channels means understanding what the process of development is about. I am afraid some rather questionable things have been done in recent years in the name of development, especially under our foreign aid programs. Before examining some of the ways in which I think we can use development assistance to promote regional cooperation in Southeast Asia, I must try, briefly, to give my own definition of development.

Development is not the same thing as economic growth. If it were, we could content ourselves with counseling poor countries to learn the right economic policies and design the right economic institutions by copying others. We could say to Indonesia, or Laos, or Cambodia, "Go to Japan or Taiwan or Korea and study the policies that the governments there have adopted and the institutions they have encouraged, for each has achieved a fantastic rate of economic growth over the past decade. Then go home and copy those policies and institutions and you, too, will grow, if not rich, at least less poor." But if we content ourselves with such preachments, our development diplomacy will certainly fail, because it will assume that economic factors are the most important factors in development. They are not. Cultural, historical, and psychological factors are just as important, if not more so. Each country, because of its special cultural and historical background, must in large part fashion its own unique development process.

While borrowing and adapting what it can from others, it must learn for itself. That is exactly what happened in Japan, Taiwan, and Korea.

For myself, I have come to define development as the process of creating room in modern technical society for some of the millions the world over who are clamoring to get in. Development assistance should be concerned with helping those who have seen the promises of modern society and have come to believe in progress but are unable to escape their historical predicament because they lack the qualifications and, usually, the opportunities as well.

Here at home, we are beginning to learn to make this kind of all-important distinction between development and economic growth. It is one lesson we are learning in our big cities today, especially from those black Americans who are demanding a position of self-respect, if not in our society, then apart from it. Few economists argue any longer that the grave problems of our cities can be solved by "fine-tuning" our economy through manipulation of fiscal and monetary policy. These are vital matters, of course; there can be no successful development without appropriate fiscal and monetary control. The "new economics," which permits us to tame the business cycle and to maintain high and stable levels of employment at high rates of growth, is certainly among the half-dozen most important social innovations of this century, but even in rich countries it is not a sufficient answer to the challenge of those who, with increasing frustration, seek equality and opportunity in modern society.

I am afraid we must accept the fact that economic growth without development will only accentuate the tensions and divisions within society. And if this is true in rich countries, how much more true it is in places like Southeast Asia. Here leaders are faced with the task of reconciling traditional attitudes toward life and work with the demands of economic growth, while at the same time having to cope with most of the competing and conflicting social demands found in rich countries.

More than a decade ago, Maurice Zinkin, now Director of Research at Lever Brothers in London and formerly a member of the Indian Civil Service, summed up the tragic dilemmas inherent in the development process. In his brilliant book *Development of Free Asia,* he wrote:

> Economic progress is sought today in Asia as elsewhere for reasons which are not economic. . . . High cost industries are built up because they are thought to contribute to national power. Amenities for labor, more expensive than productivity justifies, are enforced so that laborers shall have a better life. High incomes are taxed almost out of existence to increase equality. Location of industry is interfered with so that every part of the country shall have its "fair" share. . . . Such large farmers as know about agriculture, have their holdings cut down so that more of the landless can enjoy the pleasures of ownership.

And so on. . . . The criteria applied . . . mostly have nothing to do with economics; and the result is naturally, that though there may be more equality, or greater regional fairness or possibly fewer revolutions, there is also less development.*

If we have learned anything since Mr. Zinkin wrote this passage, it is only that we must distinguish between economic progress and development. Economic growth, or progress, is essential for development; more growth is essential to solve the problems brought on by growth in the past. But the dilemmas of development cannot be resolved simply by more economic growth. They are the result, not just of growth in the past, but of the historical impact of dynamic societies on traditional societies. This historical impact is as big a fact in world politics today as are nuclear weapons or Red China's population. It challenges all the academic disciplines and all the institutions in that part of society we call modern as much as, if not more than, any other fact of life in the twentieth century.

ECAFE

Difficult as it is to define development, controversial as is the practice of development diplomacy, the idea is one to which all nations today pay homage. That is why it is possible to point to some working models of regional

* Maurice Zinkin, *Development for Free Asia* (London: Chatto and Windus, 1956), pp. 249–50.

cooperation in Southeast Asia. There are a vast number of commissions, committees, working groups, and so on in existence today for the purpose of promoting development cooperation in the area.

Most of these organizations can trace their origin to one of the many conferences of the U.N.'s Economic Commission for Asia and the Far East. A few names of ECAFE-sponsored activities suggest the range of subjects: The Asian Coconut Community; The Committee for Coordination of Prospecting for Mineral Resources in Asian Off-shore Areas; The Meeting of Government Experts on Trade Expansion; The Working Group of Planning Experts on Regional Harmonization of Development Plans. Although all of these activities suggest a serious purpose, obviously not all of them can be taken seriously. U.N. activities are, if anything, more susceptible to Parkinson's Law of bureaucratic proliferation than are national organizations. One of the most serious problems in the international bureaucracy is how to devise ways and means of improving management and making operations more efficient. But with all its inefficiencies, ECAFE does deserve credit for having stimulated most of what is truly useful in activities designed to promote regional development cooperation.

ECAFE is also largely responsible for the most useful studies and investigations into the possibilities of regional trade cooperation. If I do not delve deeply into these

matters, it is not because I think them unimportant; it **is**
because they lie somewhat outside my subject. The important trade problems of Southeast Asia are less concerned
with regional cooperation than with the relations between
individual countries in the region and the rich countries
to which they sell their commodity exports. In the short
run, perhaps, the strictly economic future of the region is
more affected by the need for orderly and open export
markets for raw materials, such as rubber and rice, and
for light manufactures, such as textiles, than it is by the
availability of development assistance. But as yet these
trade problems do not suggest practical steps toward
regional cooperation.

Cooperation in development is another matter. Here,
by sharing experiences, pooling the scarce supply of trained
talent available, and creating channels through which
development finance from outside can flow, the nations
of the region can take and have taken practical, cooperative
initiatives. Three examples serve to suggest something of
their scope and promise.

THE ASIAN DEVELOPMENT BANK

As early as 1954, the member countries of ECAFE and
the ECAFE secretariat began talking about the formation
of an Asian development bank. I was then President of the
World Bank, and, frankly, I was opposed to the establishment of regional banks, whether in Asia or Africa or Latin

America. I feared that they would become political institutions which, while ostensibly charged with tasks very like those of the World Bank, would tend to undermine the kind of lending standards we were trying to get accepted and the confidence we were trying to build up in the bond markets of the world. I assumed then that such banks would, like the World Bank, rely on the world capital markets for the bulk of their financial resources. These markets are, after all, the largest and most flexible supply of development finance in the world.

A similar view prevailed in the U.S. Treasury Department as late as March, 1965, when at an ECAFE meeting in Wellington, New Zealand, the members of that organization appointed a consultative committee to draft a charter for an Asian development bank. The United States delegation took the position that our government would cooperate, but probably would not join. But less than a month later President Johnson, in a speech at the Johns Hopkins University in Baltimore, offered U.S. support to new, cooperative efforts to accelerate the economic and social development of the countries of Southeast Asia. The very afternoon of the day he gave that speech he asked me to become his special adviser on these matters.

My first instruction from the President was to call on U.N. Secretary General U Thant to ask him what concrete steps the United States could take then and there to signal its interest in promoting regional cooperation. The Secretary General immediately suggested support for an Asian development bank. This President Johnson agreed to, and it became my job to help establish the very institution I had once opposed.

The charter of the Asian Development Bank (ADB) was negotiated among nineteen Asian governments and thirteen governments from outside Asia, including the United States, in the remarkably brief span of a year and a half. This is a very fast clip for "institution building" in my business. Speed was possible partly because the Asians had already done a lot of the spade work, partly because the ADB's charter was modeled in large part on that of the World Bank, and partly because President Johnson had given full-speed-ahead instructions to the U.S. Government.

The ADB differs in important ways from the regional banks that have been established for Latin America and for Africa. Not surprisingly, the African Development Bank has yet to do much significant business; it was established without any donor governments among its capital subscribers. The Inter-American Development Bank, conversely, gets most of its external financial support from annual grants from the U.S. Congress under the Alliance for Progress. Virtually all of its loans are subject to the veto of the U.S. Director. This means that, whether we use it as such or not, the IADB is, first and foremost, an instrument of U.S. political policy in Latin America.

In contrast, the ADB was set up as a bank from the start. More than 60 per cent of the initial $1 billion in subscribed capital came from the nineteen Asian members; the governments from outside the region subscribed the rest. Because the ADB was founded not on a set of political assumptions but on a set of banking principles, Japan agreed to contribute $200 million to the initial capital, which sum the United States matched. The United States and Japan, together with Canada, Australia, New Zealand, and all the major Western European governments save France, constitute a majority of lenders, but Japan and the other Asian members also constitute an Asian majority. This unique combination of a big voice for the lenders and a big voice for the Asians is what distinguishes the ADB.

The Asians made it clear during negotiations that their first objective was to establish a banking institution that could get the confidence of the capital markets of the world. The charter says that at least 90 per cent of the ADB's ordinary capital resources must be loaned on conventional terms, and that means in these days at an interest rate in the neighborhood of 7 per cent. Half of the original subscriptions remain on call as security for the obligations of the bank; the other half is being paid in five equal installments in the currency of the lender. This kind of capital structure envisages relying primarily on borrowing in the world capital markets for loan funds.

During the negotiations that led to adoption of the ADB's charter, I found myself in the unaccustomed position of urging my Asian friends not to rely too heavily on conventional instruments of finance. Many countries, particularly in Southeast Asia, were in no position to borrow money on conventional terms. Others promised soon to be in a debt position that would make further borrowing on conventional terms very difficult. Finally, some of the most pressing needs, in agriculture and education particularly, seemed to me to demand finance on concessional terms. The Asians fully recognized these things, but their first interest was to see "their" bank qualify as a sound institution among those hard-nosed people who make decisions in the capital markets of the world.

A compromise was struck, which I think is a very good one. The ADB's charter authorizes the bank to receive contributions to special funds, which it may administer on terms agreed upon with the donors as long as the purposes are consistent with the bank's objectives and functions. The Japanese have already offered $100 million in five annual installments for concessional loans to agriculture, among other things; Canada has pledged $25 million over five years, and Denmark and the Netherlands have made initial contributions of $2 million and $1 million, respectively. Nearly $2 million has been contributed to the ADB's special technical assistance fund. The U.S. Congress has been asked to appropriate funds to match the Japanese contribution to the ADB's special funds.

To me, one of the most important facts about the ADB is that the Japanese have taken a leading role, both in providing finance and in providing staff. The Japanese hitherto had not taken their rightful position in international organizations; for example, during its first twenty years, the World Bank employed only two Japanese nationals. The language barrier is very serious; few among the older Japanese can speak English or any other world language well enough to work in the international civil service. The ADB, therefore, is a welcome testing ground for Japan, especially in the days ahead when Japan will be struggling with the problem of defining a new role for itself in the world. As head of their bank the Asians selected one of Japan's most distinguished financial experts, Takeshi Watanabe. President Watanabe brings to the job not only a great deal of experience in international finance, but also one of the most distinguished family names in Japan.

President Watanabe faces some very difficult problems in defining ADB's working role. The bank's membership covers a lot of geography, all the way from Afghanistan to Korea. The choice of functions on which to concentrate is as broad as the whole spectrum of development problems. Compromises, inevitably arbitrary, have to be made. India, for example, has assumed the role of lender rather than borrower at ADB, which is well, since India could absorb all of the bank's resources in a few months. The poor countries outside of Southeast Asia—Nepal, Afghanistan, and Ceylon—need special attention along with the countries of Southeast Asia. Since the real limit on the volume of development finance is not money, but sound and well-prepared projects, the ADB has to fit its role into that of the World Bank and into the operations of the various bilateral aid programs, especially that of the United States. Finally, and perhaps most difficult of all, President Watanabe has to build up his own staff, with its own competence and *esprit de corps,* in competition with all the other organizational claimants on the scarce supply of talent available. It is my guess that it will be five to seven years before the real personality of the ADB emerges. Inevitably, there will be those who will become impatient at such slow progress.

In the first two years or so after the ADB opened its doors, eleven loans, totaling $66.4 million, were made to seven countries—Ceylon, China, Korea, Malaysia, Pakistan, the Philippines, and Thailand. The projects include an expressway in Korea, financial support for industrial development banks in Thailand and Pakistan, a water supply project in Malaysia, a scheme for modernizing tea factories in Ceylon, and one for building and outfitting forty tuna fishing vessels in Taiwan. A particularly interesting loan was made to the Chinese Petroleum Corporation on Taiwan envisaging a joint marketing arrangement between Taiwan and Korea for ingredients used in the manufacture of polyester fibers.

However, these initial activities do not add up to any set policy. If the experience of the World Bank is any precedent, the ADB's set policies will grow from a staff fashioning its own definition for the word "project" and expanding that definition as it gets experience. For example, the ADB in early 1969 concluded a small technical assistance contract with the Republic of China and an American consulting firm to survey a new road from the port of Keelung in the north of Taiwan to the port of Kaohsiung, in the south. A feature of this contract, financed jointly by ADB and the Republic of China, was an agreement on the part of the American consulting firm to employ twenty-five young Chinese engineers for on-the-job training in the business of making feasibility studies (or "project preparation," as it is sometimes called). By building this on-the-job training into its financial agreement with the Chinese, the ADB was breaking new ground. The idea that training can be costed and "banked" like other capital investments is not yet accepted in the World Bank or elsewhere. If the ADB develops this technique and comes to include training costs as a matter of course as elements to be financed in its projects, it will be making a signal contribution. For in all of Asia, there is no more pressing need than to strengthen the technical competence of public services. Such competence will be very long in coming through conventional, school-oriented instruction. If the ADB can show how these costs can be absorbed in the normal course of development finance, the contribution will be far in excess of its modest resources.

One of President Watanabe's most difficult problems is going to be to carve for himself an important role in the promotion of regional cooperation in Southeast Asia without being overwhelmed by those who want the ADB to do things for which it has neither the human nor the capital resources. For example, what should be the ADB's role in postwar reconstruction and development in Vietnam? What role should the ADB play in the large cast of international characters now absorbed with Indonesia's financial problems? Should the ADB interest itself in the vast possibilities for developing the lower Mekong River basin? What should be the division of labor between the ADB and the World Bank in East Asian development?

All these questions are being asked at this writing, but I have too much respect for Takeshi Watanabe to thrust on him my own thoughts on these matters. I know from experience that the strength of an international or regional development bank depends on a strong staff and resolute management. Even the most benevolent board of directors and the most well-meaning national governments can easily make such an evolution impossible if management is not allowed to set its own course.

It may be that most of the immediately urgent problems of Southeast Asia, such as postwar reconstruction in Vietnam and stabilization in Indonesia, are too large and too pressing to permit the ADB to play a leading role at this early stage in its evolution. Just as the World Bank could never have survived had it been given the task of administering the Marshall Plan, so the ADB can easily be destroyed if too much is asked of it now. However, the ADB is one of those long-term investments in the promotion of regional cooperation which I think should be carefully nurtured and not sacrificed at the altar of emergency.

So it is with some of the other new institutions designed to serve the distant goal of regional cooperation in Southeast Asia.

Transport and Communications

For a number of years, a number of organizations have been talking about regional cooperation in transport and communications. Both the International Telecommunications Union of the United Nations and the Asian Parliamentary Union have fashioned plans for regional telecommunications networks. ECAFE's sponsorship of an Asian Highway has actually resulted in a designated road link, 94 per cent of which is already in being, running most of the breadth of Asia from Saigon to Istanbul. There has been talk of a regional shipping service, particularly among Thai officials. (Thailand set out a few years ago to establish its own overseas shipping line, but unfortunately one of the two ships in the original fleet sank on its maiden voyage.) And the United Nation's International Civil Aviation Organization has recommended a system of navigational aids and communications equipment for Southeast Asia for which, as yet, there has been neither much money nor anywhere like enough training of technical personnel.

During one of my official visits, Malaysia's energetic Deputy Prime Minister Tun Abdul Razak spoke to me of these matters and asked me if I thought Malaysia should take the lead in trying to reduce some of the many plans to workable, bankable projects. I encouraged him to do this, with a promise to recommend to my government a program of financing feasibility studies for such projects so that they could be put in a form that development bankers would have to take seriously. Out of these talks grew the Coordinating Committee of Southeast Asia Senior Officials on Transport and Communications, which for two years has been actively promoting a program of regional cooperation.

In September, 1967, eight Southeast Asian governments met in Kuala Lumpur with representatives of several international organizations and observers from a dozen governments outside the region to consider the range and number of transport and communications projects in which the Southeast Asian governments were interested. No less than ninety-five project proposals, representing an investment of more than $1 billion, were on the agenda. From the start, therefore, it was clear that priorities had to be established. The United States agreed to send a study team to look at the ninety-five proposals and to recommend from among them a group that promised truly regional benefits and could, with adequate preparation, be banked by a development finance institution. By April, 1968, the team had completed its review. Of the original proposals, sixteen were recommended for consideration by the Coordinating Committee.

The project that attracted perhaps the most attention was one suggested by Singapore involving substantial improvements to navigational aids in the Straits of Malacca, which offer the best and easiest passage for ships traveling between the Indian Ocean and the South China Sea. The port of Singapore, commanding one entrance to the Straits, is one of the most important ports in the entire Southeast Asia region. Yet at present, tankers of 200,000 tons and more cannot transit the Straits at night because navigating the channel is so tricky that insurance companies will not cover the risks of passage after dark. Improvements in the Straits of Malacca would benefit the entire region. The only problem was finding an equitable way to finance the improvements. The Japanese were naturally concerned because the Straits are on the sea highway to the Middle

East and Japan's oil supply (on any given day there is one tanker every sixty miles on the high seas between the Gulf of Aden and Japan). They seized on the proposed project immediately and offered to contribute substantially toward a program that would eventually involve clearing obstructions and dredging to a depth to accommodate the over-200,000-ton tankers that Japan is now building. In this manner, a relatively simple navigational improvement project blossomed into a sizable regional project, which may eventually involve an agreement among Malaysia, Singapore, and Indonesia to establish some sort of "Straits of Malacca Authority."

The United States and Canada came forward with offers to study the feasibility of another project selected by the study team: an area improvement program involving a new highway on Malaysia's east coast to provide a second route from the Thai border to Singapore. The new road, between the towns of Kuantan and Segamat, will connect with central markets a million acres of land slated for plantation and small-holder agricultural development. The World Bank has already made a loan for agricultural development in the region and may well finance the road project once the feasibility study is done.

The Canadians also came forward with a grant to study a second international airport at Bangkok, which has become the hub of civil aviation in Southeast Asia. The United States has promised to finance a feasibility study for a microwave communications network in Laos. At present, only the government radio connects the villages lying within that part of free Laos which stretches along the Thai border. The proposed project would, at comparatively little cost, give this area its first civilian means of radio contact and provide a connection with the multi-channel network spreading from the earth satellite station near Bangkok deep into Thailand's northeast border region.

The list of proposed projects is much longer. However, not all of them will have an easy ride to the bank. For example, one proposal for a telecommunications system to link the Malaysian states of Sabah and Sarawak, through the territory of Brunei, to the island of Mindanao in the Philippines, has temporarily run aground because of the dispute between Malaysia and the Philippines over the latter's claim to Sabah. Nevertheless, the idea of helping the governments of Southeast Asia to study the feasibility of specific regional projects in transport and communications, to bring them, where possible, to the point at which they can be taken to the bank, is one of the most effective, continuing means for the U.S. Government and other governments outside the region to promote regional cooperation.

SEAMEC

A similar opportunity exists in the field of education. The ministers of education of Southeast Asia have formed a council (SEAMEC) to explore ways of economizing, through regional cooperation, on some of their high-priority needs in higher education. The United States has committed $28 million to help SEAMEC establish a regional education center in each of five countries.

Most of the projects are attached to or are extensions of existing national centers. For example, there are plans for training teachers of mathematics and science in cooperation with the Malayan Teachers College in Penang, Malaysia, and for a program of regional agricultural studies and research in close coordination with the University of the Philippines' College of Agriculture at Los Baños in the Philippines. A center for the teaching of English as a second or foreign language has been established in Singapore. Planning is also under way for a center for educational innovation and technology, possibly in Saigon, and for a center for biological research at the National Biological Institute in Bogor, Indonesia. The largest project is the Asian Institute of Technology in Bangkok, often referred to as "the Asian MIT," governed by a fully independent board and endorsed by SEAMEC. Most SEAMEC countries provide a member for the Institute's Board of Trustees.

These new centers now serve or will soon serve to bring technicians and civil servants from the region together to work on concrete problems. The Regional English Language Center and the Asian Institute of Technology are farthest ahead and serve best to illustrate the potential in this kind of regional cooperation.

The Regional English Language Center. At the first meeting of SEAMEC in Bangkok in 1965, English language teaching was suggested repeatedly as a need suitable for regional cooperation. Throughout most of Southeast Asia, English is used as a second language and as the language of instruction in technical education, but there is a severe shortage of well-qualified English teachers and, as in all branches of education, a desperate need for newer methods and programs to stretch the supply of teachers and make them more effective.

It is only natural that in their need the countries of Southeast Asia should look for help to rich countries, particularly the United States, the acknowledged world leader in modernized education. Yet, in a sense, the rich countries set the poor countries a bad example in educational matters. There are not the resources in any country of Southeast Asia to develop a corps of teachers as we have in the United States. It is an inescapable, if lamentable, fact that no poor country anywhere in the world can afford to consume the quantity of education that goes into producing that proportion of certified teachers relative to the student population which presently exists in the United States or Europe. What is needed are new ways of teaching that economize on the use of fully certified teachers. Next to population control, this is perhaps the greatest need in poor countries today. But, as in population control, change in education is difficult, and the difficulty is as much a cultural as a technical or financial matter. In all these countries for a long time to come, both the old traditions and the new techniques and subjects will have to coexist in the schoolroom.

The English Language Center opened its doors to visiting teachers and officials from the region on September 2, 1968, when the first group of eighteen senior educators from six countries arrived in Singapore for a four-month intensive course designed to bring them up to date on the latest research and technology. In addition to taking courses in a variety of subjects, the educators did considerable research work on their own. They compared the common errors made by pupils learning English in Thailand and Singapore, suggested revisions for Indonesia's standard English-teaching guides, prepared phonological analyses of the problems involved in teaching English sounds to Malays and to Thais, and examined new teaching techniques being pioneered in Vietnam and new designs for tests and audio-visual materials being developed in the Philippines. Their reports will become part of the Center's permanent collection of materials and information on teaching methods of potential use throughout the region.

During 1968, the Center embarked upon a twelve-month field trial of a highly mechanized teacher education program. The aim was to identify the kinds of problems that can be expected to arise when sophisticated, self-instructional techniques are introduced into the largely traditional schools of Southeast Asia. The testers wanted to know something about the cost-effectiveness of the new techniques and how they might best be adapted to local conditions. The results of the field trial will help officials decide how, if at all, automated self-instructional methods can be used effectively in their local education systems.

The United States and Singapore have agreed to contribute nearly $2 million each for the construction of a sixteen-story, permanent headquarters building for the Center in Singapore and for its subsequent operation for a minimum of five years. In addition to providing lodging for about 250 educators, the building will house a library, language labs, rooms for lectures and services, audio-visual and instructional workshops, and research, publications, and conference facilities. Secretary of State William P. Rogers signed the U.S. commitment on his visit to Bangkok in May, 1969.

The Asian Institute of Technology. In the words of its official brochure, the Asian Institute of Technology (AIT) is "an independent, autonomous international institution of higher learning devoted to instruction and research in engineering and other closely related fields, to serve the region in which it is located." Increasing the supply of trained engineers is another of those glaring needs, recognized by all leaders in Southeast Asia. In the United States and most other industrialized nations, approximately one out of every 400 adults is an engineer; in Thailand, to take one Southeast Asian example, the ratio is about one to 10,000.

The Institute, which came into being in November, 1967, is a transformation of the SEATO Graduate School of Engineering, which was established by royal decree in 1959 on the campus of the Chulalongkorn University in Bangkok. The Institute has demanding standards. Dean Milton E. Bender, Jr., formerly of Colorado State University, set it up that way and is determined to keep it so. He had 465 applicants for the 1968–69 academic year, chose 227, and saw 30 per cent leave soon after they arrived. Such attrition will probably continue; standards must remain high, the trustees feel, if the AIT is to fulfill its aim of helping to stem the brain drain that afflicts all of Southeast Asia. At the same time, the standards set cannot reflect the demands of Western society, or the result may well be to accelerate the drain, rather than the opposite. Among engineering students who leave Asia to study in the United States and Europe, a great many never return. By contrast, thus far, 90 per cent of the Institute's graduates have returned to work in their own countries. The Thai Government has set an example in encouraging Thai graduates to remain in their country by offering a supplement of 200 baht ($40.00) per month to the starting salaries of those who join government service.

The Institute offers a twenty-one-month program leading

to a masters degree in engineering. Courses include civil engineering, transportation, hydraulics, soils engineering, public health engineering, structures, and coastal engineering. Most graduates so far have gone into government service, thirty-three of them into the highway departments of their respective national governments. Many AIT administrators wish that more of their graduates would go into teaching, but they expect most to go into industry, where the average graduate may start out with a salary as much as four times greater than what he would get as a teacher.

The Institute staff includes Westerners and Asians; there will soon also be a few candidates from Western countries in the student body. Dean Bender hopes that the Western influence will make itself felt in two very important ways: persuading candidates of the importance of working with their hands and encouraging the candidates to question the professor. In traditional societies, higher education is most often seen as a means of escaping manual labor; to persuade candidates that useful graduate work in engineering depends on working with one's hands is a formidable task. Traditionally, too, the social status of a professor in Asia discourages students from challenging him or even raising their hands to ask questions. At the Asian Institute of Technology, the professors are doing their best to help the students overcome this age-old diffidence. As one professor explains, "I sometimes spend the first ten minutes of class giving the students information anyone would know is wrong—complete garbage. If they still consider me infallible when I pass this stuff out, I give them hell."

Like other academic institutions, the Institute has perpetual problems with finance. Its students pay no tuition; the school covers their transportation costs to and from Bangkok and gives them living allowances while they are there. In addition to persuading governments in the region to contribute scholarships to cover these costs, Dean Bender spends a good deal of time soliciting scholarships himself from foundations and other sources within and without the region. Under his aegis, the Institute has embarked on a ten-year $15.5 million capital development program. By 1971, it hopes to be installed on a new 400-acre campus, a gift from the Thai Government; by 1977, plans call for an enrollment of 684 candidates, and a faculty of 144. The U.S. Government has promised to provide 50 per cent of the construction and operating costs. Other contributions have come from the governments of Australia, New Zealand, the Philippines, and the United Kingdom.

The Importance of Shared Experience

The diplomacy of promoting regional cooperation involves a host of activities like those described above that do not, and should not, loom large in our foreign aid budget. The results are often very small, but potentially of enduring value. For example, SEAMEC has sponsored a regional program in tropical medicine and public health, carried out under a central coordinating board in Bangkok. A prominent Malaysian doctor and medical school administrator summed up the immediate benefit of the new activities in the following way: "For the first time I can call up my colleagues in Bangkok, even send my subordinates there, without having to go through the Foreign Office."

Through a multiplicity of such contacts, officials and professional men and women in Southeast Asia are beginning to share their experiences with one another as they try to overcome more of their urgent and complex development problems. Perhaps the most useful shared experience to date has been that which the individual governments have had with the World Bank and the International Monetary Fund. A large and important group of officials in Southeast Asia has by now worked at one time or another with one or both of these institutions, negotiating loans and credits, discussing economic and monetary policies, or learning the difficult business of project preparation. Now, through the Asian Development Bank and other forums, the Asians are beginning to practice for themselves and together some of the things they learned from their experiences with the Bretton Woods institutions.

The ADB, I think, should become the development center for Southeast Asia, the place where the practical work of regional development cooperation is planned and debated. This will take time, but President Watanabe is moving in this direction now. In April, 1969, the foreign ministers of eight Southeast Asian nations and Japan, meeting in Bangkok, adopted a resolution, proposed by Thailand, asking the ADB to study the consequences for development in Southeast Asia of a number of important events: the cessation of hostilities in Vietnam and a reduction of the flow of American aid thereto; the withdrawal of British security forces from Singapore and Malaysia; and the effects in rice-producing countries of the "green revolution" in agriculture brought about by the introduction on a mass scale of new, high-yield, disease-resistant rice strains. The ADB is to report back to the foreign ministers at a meeting now scheduled for Tokyo in April of 1970. This appears to me to be a very important initiative on the part of the Asians, which, if circumstances in Vietnam permit, may be the beginning of regional cooperation on a bigger scale.

President Watanabe likes to tell visitors that he regards all Asian members of the ADB as potential lenders as well as borrowers. In this way, he is trying to encourage an atmosphere of equals working together on common problems. Certainly, if the countries of Southeast Asia and their neighbors were to begin to mobilize more of their own financial resources for productive investment, it would not only facilitate support from the United States; it would also have far-reaching effects on the stability of the region.

There are savings available in the region if they can be coaxed out of speculative investments and real estate. The first director of SEAMEC's small staff in Bangkok, Sukich Nimmanheminda, former Thai Ambassador to Washington and now Thailand's Minister of Education, likes to tell a pointed story of how, thirty years ago, King Rama IV of Thailand went about starting the Royal Thai Air Force. "The King had a tea party on the palace grounds," Ambassador Sukich says. "He invited all the leading families of Bangkok. At the end of the party he assigned each family the cost of one airplane. That's how our Air Force got its first thirty-two fighters."

SEAMEC's primary function is to persuade the official families of Southeast Asia's education ministries to make contributions to regional education projects. Obviously, the Council will be more persuasive if it can also raise some funds from governments and private sources overseas. Still, the idea of regional fund-raising activities is an apt one for many fields. It is a good way of engaging the elites of Southeast Asia in works of regional cooperation.

The diplomacy of regional cooperation in the period after the end of hostilities in Vietnam should involve many variations on these themes, and a good deal of American involvement should take place outside official channels.

As I will argue in Chapter VI, the U.S. Government cannot substitute its development strategy for that of the governments of Southeast Asia any more than it can substitute American soldiers for theirs in maintaining internal security. Disengagement should mean a rapid reduction in the official U.S. presence in the region, but it should also mean a considerable substitution of unofficial contacts between American universities, businesses, and foundations and the various groups of Asians interested in working on some of the many tasks of regional cooperation.

The big task for the U.S. Government is to change the image of our policy in substantial and constructive ways. We cannot ignore the effect of our own excessive involvement of recent years. Even as we adopt a much more modest stance, we have to somehow rekindle confidence among our friends. Fortunately, there is an exceptional opportunity open to us.

V

The Mekong Basin:
Vision and Opportunity

THERE ARE compelling reasons why the United States should try to balance the effects of disengagement in Vietnam with a new, positive program. Clearly, we have an obligation to help with the reconstruction of that sorely tried country. Also, liquidation of the Vietnam war and a general reduction of our military presence in Southeast Asia is bound to create widespread doubts about our resolve to defend our real national interests there.

President Nixon has made it clear in his writings and speeches that he believes that the United States has a vital interest in preventing domination of the region by one country, but giving effect to this interest after hostilities cease in Vietnam is going to demand acts of high statesmanship. At this writing, we do not know what kind of government we will be dealing with in Saigon after hostilities have ceased. We do not even know whether there will be a formal end to the war, or simply a gradual, unilateral withdrawal of American troops as the South

Vietnamese armies are able to shoulder more of the fighting themselves. The bureaucracy in Washington has not yet received any substitute instruction to take the place of "win the war"; regrettably, it is as true now as it has been since World War II that the federal government still finds it very difficult to plan for peace in time of war. However, assuming that disengagement does not simply mean renouncing any vital interest in the affairs of Southeast Asia, the kind of new instruction that the bureaucracy is likely to get from President Nixon is not hard to imagine.

Disengagement almost certainly will mean finding ways and means of using U.S. influence to evoke responsibility and responsiveness among the nations of the region so that they can, preferably by working together, cope with more of their own problems themselves. This theme pervades the report recently presented to South Vietnam's President Nguyen Van Thieu by David Lilienthal, who has been working with a group of South Vietnamese officials on the problems of postwar reconstruction in that country. He has explored in great detail the difficulties and opportunities that Vietnam will face in converting to a peacetime economy after more than two decades of war. He and his South Vietnam colleagues found that Vietnam has great economic assets, which can be used to bring about a strong recovery in a relatively short time. They estimate that perhaps $2.5 billion in external finance, spread over ten years, will be needed to bring about such a recovery. They recommend the establishment of an *ad hoc* consortium of interested governments to provide this capital, perhaps with the Asian Development Bank serving as secretariat for the consortium.

This is not the place to examine in detail the economic problems of reconstruction in Vietnam. Suffice it to say that the Vietnamese economy is now totally dependent on U.S. finance. The U.S. military is injecting hundreds of millions of dollars each year to pay for services it needs. The Agency for International Development is supplying hundreds of millions of dollars each year to stem inflation and to pay for contractors' fees and technical assistance services of various kinds. I will have some very general observations in the next chapter concerning how the United States might shift its operations when reconstruction can start in earnest in Vietnam. Here, however, I am particularly interested in what Lilienthal and his colleagues have to say about the Mekong delta in South Vietnam and how its development could be tied into the development plans of neighboring countries to give a regional scope to policies in the postwar period.

The major development scheme proposed by Lilienthal is a thirty- to forty-year program of water control in the Mekong delta. The aim of the program is to help Vietnam to become one of the world's largest producers of rice through introduction of the new miracle varieties and through a series of levees and upstream reservoirs designed to control the flow of the floodwater in the delta. He urges the South Vietnamese Government to make a start on this program in 1970. Increased food production is certain to be a number one priority in any reconstruction program; if the delta is developed along the lines proposed by the Lilienthal group, South Vietnam a decade from now may be feeding millions beyond its borders.

The delta project suggests to me an opportunity for tying the work of reconstruction in Vietnam into a regional program capable of giving concrete expression to the objective of promoting regional cooperation. It suggests to me a way of designing a U.S. policy to substitute engagement in development for engagement in armed conflict, not just in Vietnam, but in Laos, Thailand, and Cambodia as well.

Development of the lower Mekong basin offers the most dramatic kinds of prospects. Even one large hydroelectric dam on the main stream would permit the building of a power grid connecting the capitals of the four riparian countries—including Hanoi, if North Vietnam were interested. The same dam could by itself provide a sufficient increase in the flow of water during the dry season in the Mekong delta to permit double-cropping, with a consequent vast increase in the production of rice and of crops of higher value. For the future of Vietnam, such a development would mean the creation of a hinterland market without which much of the war-born investment in that country, particularly the investment in harbors and airfields, will simply have to be written off.

Most important, if the energies and resources of the international community can be engaged in such a program, it will inhibit violence in this troubled and dangerous corner of the world through the construction of hydroelectric dams, irrigation schemes, and ancillary projects. It would evoke among these countries a sense of what is possible if they cultivate the habit of working together. By treating the lower Mekong basin as a single development unit, and by working with and through appropriate regional and international organizations, the United States can hold out the possibility of replacing the costly, dangerous, and highly uncertain business of American involvement in counterinsurgent warfare with American involvement in an internationally sponsored Mekong development program.

In other words, the Mekong basin affords us the opportunity to join the rational and moral dimensions of our foreign policy in a manner, if not on a scale, that has not been possible since the Marshall Plan.

THE RIVER DEVELOPMENT CONTROVERSY

Before examining what a Mekong development program would entail, I have to recognize that multipurpose river development has become a latter-day controversy inside the United States, even as Americans have planted the idea the world over that modern nations should control their great rivers.

We have taught hundreds of engineers in poor countries to think of the tremendous benefits a river can yield once its flow is regulated by man. Each year in recent years, an average of 2,500 engineers and government officials from abroad have visited the Tennessee Valley Authority (TVA) to learn how we make a river system produce electricity and potable water for cities and municipalities; how we store flood waters and rob them of their power to devastate land; how we alter the contour of rivers so that ships can ply farther upstream; how we "colonize" fish in river sanctuaries so that they can multiply more freely; how we curry the river banks and lake shores into recreation parks. Visitors who have gone on to visit the Columbia River basin and Grand Coulee and Bonneville dams have seen how, by storing the waters of great rivers in an integrated system of reservoirs, vast acreages of dry land have been irrigated to provide bumper harvests.

But at the same time we have been exhibiting to others the achievements of our dam builders, here at home we have come to question some of what they have achieved. Virtually all of the suitable natural sites in our country have been developed. Meanwhile, we have reached that plateau of affluence where the conservationist's voice is heard ever louder in the land and is getting a deserved audience. More and more, we have to pay attention to the conservation of our natural resources, rather than their exploitation, to worry about problems of environmental pollution and encroachments on our wilderness areas. We have even begun to preach to the poor countries about these problems.

To my mind, however, there is something rather arrogant about exporting this kind of controversy. Certainly, to plan the wisest use of untapped resources even in a poor country we should mobilize the ecologists and the social scientists along with the engineers and the economists. But we should bear in mind, too, that if the poor countries do not exploit what they have, the only thing they will be able to conserve is their poverty. They have their own problems of environmental pollution, but they are not the same as ours. It would be tragic if we were to deny them their opportunities to develop their natural resources simply because we face a set of problems, essentially the problems of affluence, that we have not yet solved.

There is an equal and opposite argument in the river development controversy. It is that it is wrong to bring visitors from poor countries to the TVA because only rich countries can afford to tame their rivers the way we do. Only in countries where capital is relatively cheap and there are extraordinary demands for electric power can the huge constuction costs and long amortization periods be borne; the biggest user of TVA power (still only accounting for a small fraction of the total) is the atomic energy installation at Oak Ridge. One could say it would make much more sense to take visitors from poor countries to the New York Stock Exchange, where domestic savings are mobilized for a dazzling array of lesser investments in development. After all, the first development requirement in poor countries is to persuade people to save for productive investment.

However, this problem to some extent has been provided for. After World War II, new kinds of organizations, like the World Bank, were established to make capital available to poor countries at reasonable rates for such investments as multipurpose river development projects. This did not, by any means, eliminate the controversy. It remains true that in all countries, rich and poor, decisions to allocate resources on the scale of multipurpose river development projects are highly controversial. But that the nations of the world want such decisions, and for good reasons, is obvious. One might as well argue that the United States should keep secret the astronauts' trips in outer space as argue that multipurpose river development is a bad thing. Our dam builders are, in fact, the linear ancestors of our astronauts; the older generation's ability to tame rivers is of a piece with the new generation's ability to conquer space. The world wants to learn from the technology that made these things possible, not necessarily so that others can go to the moon, but so that others can live better here on earth.

Advances in technology may sharpen the controversy over multipurpose river development projects, but they can never by themselves resolve it. This kind of decision can only be made at high political levels. Politicians should be informed with as much technical knowledge as possible in as orderly a way as possible, before decisions are made. But it would be tragic for the rich countries to impose on the poor countries procedures that reflect more of the problems of affluence than of poverty.

And in talking about river development in poor countries, there is another, overriding factor to consider. Multipurpose river development projects can play an important part in keeping the peace. Let me give a few illustrations of where this overriding political factor has served to resolve the technical controversy in very useful ways.

RIVERS FOR PEACE

The Zambezi River in Africa was first dammed at Kariba, between present-day Rhodesia and neighboring Zambia. In a sense, the dam joins the two countries, while the river separates them. Kariba was a sound economic proposition. The coal mines, now in Zambia, were not producing enough to feed the rich Rhodesian copper belt, and industry was growing at a rapid pace in what was then Southern Rhodesia. There was a demonstrable demand for a large, new source of power. But when the World Bank, in partnership with the British Government and other public and private interests, agreed to finance Kariba, we also hoped that the project would serve to cement the fledgling Federation of Rhodesia and Nyasaland. We were to be disappointed: the Federation foundered on the rocks of racial politics. But not Kariba. It operates today at about 80 per cent of capacity, the only functioning link between black Zambia and the white Rhodesian Government. Both parties gain too much from Kariba to permit its immobilization.

Kariba was a sound economic proposition. The division of the waters of the Indus River system between Pakistan and India was politics from beginning to end.

The Indus plans were drawn up by General Raymond A. "Speck" Wheeler, who came to the World Bank in 1947 after retiring as chief of the U.S. Army Corps of Engineers. As General Wheeler says, "The idea of dividing one river system into two violated all the engineering principles of my lifetime." After six years of on-and-off-again negotiations, the governments of India and Pakistan adopted General Wheeler's plan because they believed that without a division of the Indus waters a disastrous war between the two countries would be inevitable. As President of the World Bank at the time, I was quite persuaded of this, as were the several member governments of the Bank, especially the United States, that contributed finances to the Indus scheme.

War did break out between India and Pakistan in September, 1965. One sharp battle was fought near Lahore, in West Pakistan, close by the site of the Mangla Dam, a major new dam being built under the Indus scheme. The battle occurred at the most crucial point in a dam-builder's schedule: the moment of closure. That is the time when the diversion tunnels are plugged because enough construction has taken place to permit blockage of the river and build-up of the reservoir. On a dam site, everybody always works around the clock at closure. Supplies have to arrive right on time. And arrive they did, even though they had to pass through the ranks of the Pakistani army while it was engaged in battle. I think it quite possible that fear of the potential damage to the Indus scheme helped to prevent an all-out war between the two countries.

Then there is the Aswan Dam. I have never made a secret of the fact that the greatest disappointment in my life was when Secretary of State John Foster Dulles, after encouraging the World Bank to take on this project on the Nile River in Egypt, withdrew the support of the U.S. Government at the last minute. This was a decision with which I thoroughly disagreed. My worst fears were realized almost immediately when, whether as a consequence or not, President Gamal Nasser nationalized the Suez Canal and invited the Russians to build Aswan. I still think we would be somewhat better off now in the Middle East if the World Bank and the United States and its allies had helped build the dam instead of Russia. But without U.S. financial participation, that was impossible.

The Aswan Dam is no longer just a Russian investment in Egypt; it is one of the few, fragile investments in peace in the Middle East. Aswan did not prevent a war in June, 1967; it is hardly sufficient to serve as a basis for negotiation between Arab and Israeli. But the existence of Aswan, like the existence of Kariba and of the Indus scheme, does inhibit extreme violence. I suspect its deterrent quality is understood very well in both Tel Aviv and Cairo.

The decision to go ahead with the Kariba, Indus, and Aswan schemes was in each case essentially political. So great are the resources involved in multipurpose projects, so many the uncertainties born of very long lead times for construction and ancillary development, that even for projects within the United States we look to a political body to make the key decisions; the U.S. Senate decides on our own multipurpose river development projects, enshrining in law the portion of the cost to be assessed to the specific benefits that the project is designed to produce. Each of the international schemes above was supported by masses of data and technical argument. Each was preceded by months or years of preparation and negotiation among the financial participants. But a political decision determined when construction started. For the Indus scheme, several governments, in addition to the World Bank, joined to make the necessary decision, as the British Government and the World Bank had for Kariba. In the case of Aswan, the U.S. Government, on political grounds, decided not to help; the Russian Government, also on political grounds, decided otherwise.

Those nations interested in stability and security in Southeast Asia now have in the lower Mekong basin another opportunity to make a river work for peace. But there must first be a major political decision.

THE MEKONG

The Mekong is the most important international river in the world that has never been restrained, nor even bridged, by man. It rises on the Great Tibetan Plateau, forms the border of Burma with Laos for one hundred miles, divides Laos from Thailand for almost all of their long common frontier, plunges into the heart of Cambodia, and, after a journey of 2,600 miles, enters the South China Sea through the "nine dragons' mouths" in the Mekong delta of South Vietnam.

Men have had visions of developing the Mekong for decades. The guardians of those visions today form an unusual group, called the Mekong Committee, which has its headquarters in Bangkok and an expert staff paid for by the United Nations. This Committee, founded in 1957, is governed by one representative each from Laos,

Cambodia, Thailand, and Vietnam. Half of the staff comes from the riparian countries; half are foreign experts, who still work, after more than a decade, under "temporary" contract to the United Nations. At the head of the staff is an American, Hart Schaaf, once of Cornell University, who for more than ten years now has been the chief world salesman for Mekong development.

The Mekong Committee has a statute to which the four riparian governments subscribed. Committee members envision that their statute will one day evolve into a charter for a "Lower Mekong Basin Authority." Right now, the idea sounds more than a little ambitious. But that does not detract from the fact that the Committee has performed an amazing political function. First, while the four riparian governments have bickered and fought with one another over other matters (Cambodia does not even have diplomatic relations with Thailand and Vietnam), the Committee members have continued to meet three or four times a year to talk about their river. Second, they have raised over $100 million from 26 different countries, 15 international organizations, 4 private foundations, and a number of private business enterprises. This money, only one-third of which has come from the United States, has been spent to study the Mekong's flow, to identify possible damsites on tributaries and on the main stream, and to learn about the livelihoods of the 25 million people in the 4 riparian countries who live indentured to the capricious temper of the Mekong. Nearly half of the money raised from outside sources has been donated by the riparian countries themselves. Four tributary dams are under construction. Two others have been completed.

It was my good fortune, while serving as President Johnson's adviser, to participate with the Mekong Committee in bringing to the point of construction its first projects in Laos and Cambodia. Since two projects had already been completed in Thailand, a special effort was devoted to preparing a project in Laos and one in Cambodia. The Committee is anxious to impress on each member country that all will benefit from its works; it wants its next project to be a bridge over the Mekong in South Vietnam. This strategy of assuring fair shares to each riparian country was absolutely necessary to gain local support for the Mekong idea. One could say that the primary function of the Mekong Committee has been to establish political priorities.

The project in Laos is a small hydroelectric dam at a spot on a tributary of the Mekong called Nam Ngum. Since Laos at this time had no credit standing at all, a $30 million fund for the dam was donated by the United States, which contributed 50 per cent, and Australia, New Zealand, Japan, Thailand, France, the Netherlands, Canada, and Denmark. The funds were deposited with the World Bank, which agreed to act as fiscal agent, making sure that the monies were spent for the right things and that construction was carried out in a competent manner. This turned out to be a new kind of job for the World Bank. Nam Ngum is being built in a region where the practitioners of counterinsurgency are hard at work. The Communist Pathet Lao can disrupt work at the dam-site any time they want; they have, on one occasion, lobbed a mortar shell into a quarry being mined for the dam's foundation. All in all, it is not the sort of place a sound banker of dams would care to put his money.

Yet the dam will be built, barring only the most un-likely of circumstances. Prince Souvanna Phouma of Laos has agreed with his Communist half-brother, Prince Souphanouvong, that it should be built. The contractor is a Japanese firm; after the one incident at the quarry, the Pathet Lao representative in the Laotian capital of Vientiane assured the Japanese Embassy there on several occasions that his army did not intend to impede construction at the damsite. No one can guarantee, of course, that Nam Ngum will not end up producing electricity for a Communist government in Vientiane, but the practitioners of counterinsurgency cannot guarantee that their game will work either. There is just as much chance that Nam Ngum, as a symbol of what can be achieved through international cooperation, may play a significant part in bringing about a cease-fire between the warring factions and encouraging them to patch up their differences. At least, it can be said that, when the Japanese contractor finishes the job of building the dam, it will inhibit anybody who wants to tear it down. A good part of the electricity from Nam Ngum will be sold to Thailand, some in return for power now being supplied to Vientiane by the Thais under the Nam Ngum agreement. The Asian Development Bank has already let a contract to survey the Vientiane plain for agricultural projects in Laos, which can be serviced by the power and the waters of Nam Ngum.

The Mekong Committee's first project in Cambodia is on a tributary of the main stream called Prek Thnot. I had hoped that the U.S. Government would contribute to this project, too, but it turned out to be impossible while American soldiers in Vietnam were being fired on from Cambodian territory (though not by Cambodians). Perhaps it is just as well, for the Japanese agreed to take the lead with Prek Thnot. They put up one-third of the $27 million needed; western European countries and India and Pakistan are putting up one-third; and Cambodia itself, the remainder. Although the United States was the original promoter of Prek Thnot outside the region, the project is going ahead without U.S. participation.

The United Nations has appointed a special coordinator, an Englishman, to act as fiscal agent for Prek Thnot. He resides in Cambodia's capital, Phnom Penh, and his job is to see to it that the contractor, again a Japanese firm, gets from the Cambodian and other governments the supplies and labor he needs. When the project is complete, the

Mekong Committee will have shown that it is capable of fashioning some rather imaginative administrative arrangements in a part of the world where suspicion still rules.

The immediate goal of the Mekong Committee is to dam the mighty main stream itself. As early as 1957, the Committee asked the World Bank to let them have General Wheeler to head a team to pick a site. They wanted, they said, "a water engineer, because on water things we can get people to talk to one another around here." General Wheeler floated down the Mekong in a small boat, like Marquette and Joliet on the Mississippi. He had with him a Chinese, a Frenchman, a Canadian, an Indian, and a Japanese, as well as his hosts from the Mekong Committee staff. As he tells the story, "There were no maps of the country; we had to make them. Nobody had any data on the river flow, or even any idea how to keep data. What I saw was a truly virgin river. Such sights disappeared in our country long before I was born."

General Wheeler's party, in addition to calling for a basin-wide development plan, suggested several sites for main-stream dams; the favored was Pa Mong, between Laos and Thailand. His original 1957 suggestion has been supported by $10 million worth of studies since. By the time these words appear, a detailed feasibility study of the project will have been completed by the largest team of U.S. Bureau of Reclamation engineers ever assembled overseas. Team Leader Lyle Mabbott is quite sure that "somebody is going to build that dam someday." But who? And how? And when?

CAN-DO ENGINEERS AND
DOUBTING-THOMAS ECONOMISTS

Building the Pa Mong, if it is ever done, will be a giant undertaking. The reservoir created by the dam will form a lake in Laos and northeast Thailand one quarter the size of Lake Erie. In its first stage, the dam will have an installed capacity of 2.8 million kilowatts; at full capacity, it will generate 50 per cent more power than is generated at Grand Coulee and two and one-half times that generated at Aswan. This power supply, in conjunction with that from other projects now under construction or proposed, will permit a power grid connecting Saigon, Pnom Penh, Bangkok, Vientiane, and Hanoi. Water stored at Pa Mong, more than 1,000 miles upstream from the Mekong delta, will provide substantial flood control and navigation benefits, will greatly increase the power output of dams downstream, and will fully meet the need for irrigation water in the delta—all this in addition to making possible the supply of irrigation waters to up to 5 million acres of dry land around the damsites.

Today, the estimated cost of Pa Mong is in the neighborhood of $1 billion. But it will take three years just to prepare detailed engineering plans for the dam and another seven or eight years to build it. By then, the cost may actually be much higher. The engineers who have been studying the project believe that it will provide power more economically than atomic energy, which is the cheapest alternative. In fact, the initial studies of the Bureau of Reclamation justify the benefits of Pa Mong on power alone, ignoring potential benefits from irrigation, flood-control, navigation, and so forth.

The economist who works for a development bank is bound to question these projections. Thailand, which would be the biggest user of Pa Mong power, has an installed capacity of only 600,000 kilowatts of electricity now. It cannot wait until some time in the 1980's for the power to be turned on at Pa Mong. Yet if new power capacity—including nuclear power, which Thailand may decide to install in two years' time—is built, how can Thailand absorb 2.8 million kilowatts coming on stream all at once in the early 1980's? Power demand in Thailand has been increasing at the phenomenal rate of nearly 30 per cent annually in recent years, but, considering the impact of the Vietnam war, is it reasonable to expect the demand for power to grow at this rate through the 1980's and beyond? It will take many millions of dollars of additional "user" investment to justify such a large investment in power. Will it be forthcoming? Are there not better investment opportunities in Thailand and Laos for the capital that Pa Mong will absorb?

This kind of argument between the can-do engineer and the doubting Thomas economist is a feature of all large, multipurpose projects. Over the years since the Reclamation Bureau first started to make rudimentary cost/benefit studies in 1902, the argument has grown more and more complicated as ever more new costs and benefits have been added to the equation. The procedures for balancing the cost/benefit equation are at best imperfect. For example, the engineers, in designing a dam, do not even have a common agreement on what constitutes failure of the structure against which engineering tolerances have to be measured. The economists have nothing like the amount of historical experience needed to make their projections of demand more than educated guesses. But the procedures are vitally important, nonetheless, for the resources going into a project like Pa Mong are enormous. If the result were to be a modern Ozymandias, whose "vast and trunkless legs of stone" stood in the desert, then the world would certainly look upon these works and despair.

One thing we can always be fairly sure of: the reality will differ from that predicted by the cost/benefit study. Twelve years ago, when I was President of the World Bank, we made our first power loan in Thailand. It was a large loan, $66 million, for a dam on the Chao Phraya River above Bangkok. My friends in the bond market in New York let me know discreetly that they thought this a rather large loan for a country like Thailand. But the market estimates for the project looked good. My experts in the World Bank, grave and conservative men, were quite confident that by the early 1960's peak power demand would be rising at a healthy 8 to 10 per cent each year in Bangkok and 5 per cent in the countryside. Nobody could say much about the likely effects on rice production; like all good agricultural economists, mine were warning me that the mere provision of water does not mean that farmers will use it well or will agree to move to cultivate new land made arable by the provision of irrigation waters. Accordingly, the Bank assessed all the costs of this project to power, and the loan was made.

Ten years after that decision, the demand on Thailand's power system was growing at the rate of 29 per cent a year, not 10 per cent as had been predicted. Thanks in part to water control, rice yields on the central Thai plain doubled in the 1960's. Thanks to the dam and an accompanying downstream barrage, second cropping is now possible, and profitable, on 500,000 acres in the central plain.

This project sounds successful, but it was not in all respects. The hydrological data used in the appraisal were quite inadequate. Much too short a period of years was studied, and only one-third the volume of water predicted by the engineers is flowing into the reservoir today. As a result, officials in charge of the Chao Phraya power authority have been regularly squeezed between the demands of politicians who want water released for irrigation and the demand for water for electric power. The power generated at a hydroelectric dam depends on the volume of water in the reservoir, the rate of flow through the reservoir, and the head of water above the turbine intakes. This year, even after stopping all special releases of water for irrigation, the level in the reservoir is only inches above the turbine intakes. Power shortages in Bangkok will result.

Moreover, since all the costs of the Chao Phraya project were assessed to power and none to the farmers who benefited from the project, the financial structure of the Thai power authority is weaker today than it should be. The loan has to be paid off even though there is not enough water to maintain a full power supply. In the best of circumstances, it is very difficult to persuade a peasant farmer in Southeast Asia that he should pay for water. The usual tactic is to try to persuade him that he should pay for the facilities that bring the water to him—the irrigation canals and other works connected with irrigation. But this has not yet been done successfully anywhere in Thailand; there, as in other countries, the preferred way of taxing the peasant farmer is through indirect taxes.

Even though Pa Mong could be justified, theoretically, on power benefits alone, I do not believe it would be wise to charge the full cost to any single benefit. The TVA would never have been built had only one benefit been considered. In fact, TVA was on the verge of dying on the drawing boards until the late Senator George Norris of Nebraska persuaded the architects to think bigger, to think of the multiplicity of potential benefits, and then set about justifying the project on a broader base. So, I believe, it will have to be with Pa Mong.

THE OPPORTUNITY

Considering all the uses for its waters, and considering the lower Mekong basin as a whole, there is sound justification for Pa Mong. But this is of less immediate importance than the diplomatic opportunity afforded by consideration of this project in the context of a comprehensive lower Mekong basin development program, one that would include the Lilienthal project in the Mekong delta of South Vietnam, a regional electric power grid, and other tributary and main stream projects, especially those in Cambodia and Vietnam, now being studied under the auspices of the Mekong Committee. This opportunity demands serious consideration by our diplomats in the State Department, even more than by the engineers and the economists. If we are to substitute Mekong development for our involvement in counterinsurgent warfare, the first need is for a diplomacy to fit the decision.

This is not to suggest that the U.S. Government should simply offer to move in and start building on the Mekong. Quite the opposite. What I think the Asians want, and what we should want, too, is much greater finesse on the part of the Americans, much more patience, much more understanding, much less pressure. This means reducing promptly and sharply, when possible, the proliferation of American official presences in Vietnam, Thailand, and Laos, and substituting a multilateral framework for our policy. The fact that such diverse countries as Japan, Sweden, and France are among the two dozen countries that have already shown an active interest in Mekong development encourages me to think that in this case a strong multilateral framework can be devised.

The diplomatic problem is to reconcile with the short-term needs and demands of the riparian countries the long-range interest that the rest of the world has in restoring peace and stability in this area. Mekong development offers the opportunity to protect this interest by building inhibitions in the form of development projects among four fragmented countries that are likely to find themselves beset with turmoil and threats for some time to come. Mekong development is an invitation to North Vietnam to join in a vast program of regional cooperation. It is just the sort of commitment needed to counteract the ill-effects of the Vietnam war.

The United States should be willing to share in such a commitment, if only to show the world that we have learned the real lesson of the Vietnam war, that we know it is futile to try to solve, all at once, problems that are certain to be with us for a long time. By moving Mekong development to the center of our diplomacy in this part of Asia, we will, I hope, be expressing confidence in the people there and encouraging them to renew their confidence in us.

It will not be easy to make such a policy credible among the four riparian countries. Both the Thais and the Vietnamese are likely to suspect talk of Mekong development as being simply a way for the Americans to back out of other commitments. We cannot pretend that more than a tiny group of officials in these countries understand even the rudiments of multipurpose river-basin development. But if the United States uses its influence to encourage other governments, particularly Japan and the governments of Western Europe, to take leading roles in Mekong development, it should be possible over time to create a new spirit in the riparian countries.

The United States cannot assign roles to other governments in Mekong development, reserving to itself the controlling decisions. We will have to adopt what the Japanese call a "low posture" and exercise a discreet influence, largely by working with and through appropriate regional and international organizations. In any case, the problems of development in the Mekong basin are so many and so complicated that it would be quite unrealistic for the United States to undertake the job alone. It would be futile for us to try to supply the finance, management, and administrative competence needed to plan, build, and operate projects on the Mekong ourselves. The necessary competence must be built up within the region over many years. Main-stream projects on the Mekong will require devising new kinds of international authorities, capable both of managing operations and of attracting the necessary development capital. This requirement alone suggests a lengthy and unique international negotiation that may take several years.

What is needed first from the United States is a firm commitment to the Secretary General of the United Nations, to the Mekong Committee, to the Asian Development Bank, and to the World Bank to help in every way it can to fashion the kinds of organizations needed to make a reality out of the vision of Mekong development. This may mean supplying technical assistance and finance to the Mekong Committee to enable it to become a continuing center of planning and research for the lower Mekong basin. It may mean helping to equip this Committee eventually to direct such common services as flood warning and navigational aid programs, to encourage the integration of national development planning within the four riparian countries, and to strengthen its fund-raising potential generally.

The World Bank, perhaps in partnership with the Asian Development Bank, might be encouraged to act as the agent of the Mekong Committee in several important matters. The World Bank has already offered to make legal assistance available to the Committee in its efforts to devise a treaty and ultimately an authority or authorities governing main-stream projects like Pa Mong. It might also offer to provide the Committee with a small team of analysts to assist in the development of project proposals and to carry out feasibility studies on tributary projects. The World Bank might undertake to appraise the justifications for main-stream projects like Pa Mong and, ultimately, be the agent for bringing together finance for such projects and for supervising construction.

The Diplomatic Role of the United States

The diplomatic role of the United States will be vitally important in all these matters—provided that Mekong development is made a centerpiece of our new policy. The decisions involved are too complex to be left to low-level civil servants in the State Department or the Agency for International Development. They warrant, I think, the appointment of a special ambassador, directly responsible to the Secretary of State. The role of this man would be to coordinate the varied American inputs to a Mekong development program and to represent the United States in negotiations with other governments and international organizations that participate in the program.

The United States should be generous in its offers to finance various aspects of the program, but initially the finance required will not be very great. For example, it will cost as much as $50 million to produce detailed engineering drawings and building specifications for a project like Pa Mong. If asked, I think the United States should be willing to offer to the World Bank half of that sum to hire U.S. experts for such a task. The World Bank would then bring together an international engineering consortium to do the job.

There may be several cases like this where finance is needed for planning, project preparation, and feasibility studies. Funds should be available on flexible enough terms so that U.S. officials can use them either for bilateral assistance or assistance through a regional or international organization. But even if the costs of building Pa Mong are included, our contribution over many years would not be greater than the cost of a few weeks of war in Vietnam.

Perhaps most important, the whole complex process of preparing for Mekong development should include training and strengthening of the civil administrations in the riparian countries. Participation should be the rule in every operation. This seems almost a platitude, but it is surprising how often opportunities to encourage participation are ignored. For example, the Bureau of Reclamation team now conducting a feasibility study for Pa Mong hired 200 Thai "driver-technicians" on the open market to help with the survey work. The wage paid is twice that paid by the Royal Thai Irrigation Department for similar work. Team Leader Lyle Mabbott is concerned about this because he does not know what will happen to his 200 Thai employees when the study is completed. When a friend of mine asked Mabbott why he had not negotiated with the Thai authorities to take on 200 low-level Thai civil servants who could have been trained on the job, and at less cost, and with the prospect of continuing employment, he answered, "My instructions were to gather data fast. Nobody said anything about training." This was a missed opportunity of a kind that happens all too often. If we are really to help these countries help themselves, then training deserves equal billing with data collection. I am afraid our diplomacy will surely fail, as it has so often under our foreign aid programs, if we simply do the work ourselves.

A distinguished diplomat, a colleague of mine in the World Bank, used to say that in diplomacy it is not the wisdom of the advice given that really counts; rather, it is the willingness of others to accept wise advice. The point applies very well in the context of Mekong development. This proposal will not work if it appears as just another pet project of the Americans. It will look even worse if it appears to Asians and Europeans as a means of involving them in "clearing up the mess in Vietnam"—a mess which many think is of American making.

What the vision of Mekong development provides is an opportunity to change our policy image in a part of the world where the competing ambitions and suspicions of Thais, Vietnamese, Laotians, and Cambodians tempt others with a vested interest to stir up trouble and where we, in the eyes of too many people, now have the reputation of trouble-maker.

VI

Policy for a New Era

IT IS SAD, I think, that the era in American history that started with the New Deal and ended with Lyndon Johnson has not been given the honorable burial it deserves. For whatever one's politics, those were momentous years when much was achieved of which all Americans ought to be proud.

One could make a pretty good case for saying that the New Deal years ended on the streets of Chicago during the Democratic Party Convention in August, 1968, for there the children of the New Deal came into direct conflict with those who had benefited most from and had provided much of the leadership during the New Deal years. It was a tragedy that no Mark Anthony appeared on the scene to remind us that "the evil that men do lives after them; the good is oft interred with their bones."

One could say that the foreign policies of the New Deal and the Fair Deal, the Eisenhower years, and the New Frontier came to their end in Vietnam. And again it is a tragedy that no one has come forward to bury those policies with the honors they deserve.

But that an era has ended, no one can doubt. The symbolic events are less important than the new awareness about the human condition that has been gradually borne in upon us. Nothing marks the end of the New Deal era more certainly than our incipient awareness that there is no substitute for diplomacy in the affairs of nations and that development is not the same thing as economic growth.

If there is to be more peace and less war on this planet, we are going to have to practice diplomacy more expertly than ever before, and we are going to have to promote something called development as a means of accommodating more of the millions in the world who are struggling to get a foothold in modern, technical society. We are going to have to create the opportunities and teach the qualifications for more of these millions, and this requires much more than a concern for economic growth. As the mayor of St. Louis observed not so long ago, we who enjoy the fruits of modern society cannot simply hang out signs saying "the uneducated need not apply" and expect to keep intruders from our doors.

In these pages, I have tried to test these propositions in the context of Southeast Asia. What the United States does in Southeast Asia in the two or three years immediately ahead will determine in large part whether the new era in foreign policy starts on a constructive note or on a note of defeatism. Our own self-confidence as a world power and the confidence of our friends and allies in the region are at stake.

THE OPPORTUNITIES

In order to substitute the promotion of regional co-operation for our present over-involvement in the affairs of the nations of Southeast Asia, good diplomacy demands that we first understand where our real opportunities lie. They are not dramatic opportunities, such as were presented to us during the reconstruction of Western Europe under the Marshall Plan. However, we must make use of such opportunities as do exist if we are not to manufacture our own defeat as a result of our unhappy experience in Vietnam.

I list the opportunities this way:

1. The leaders of Southeast Asia share a fear of domination by Communist China and a suspicion of Japan. Because of their fears and suspicions, they feel that they need a U.S. presence in the region. This is the major reason why we can talk seriously about a U.S. role in promoting regional cooperation.

2. The promotion of regional cooperation offers one of the few constructive opportunities open to us in Southeast Asia in the years immediately ahead to reconcile

our diplomacy with that of Japan. The Japanese say that they do not want to see an Asia divided into "our side and the other side," as Americans have become accustomed to saying. They will talk about a "unified Asia" as long as they are going through the trauma of determining anew a role for themselves in the world. Neither of these rhetorical positions is very realistic, however necessary either may be for home consumption in the two countries. Asia can neither be unified nor pushed into choosing sides. We can hope to persuade the Japanese, however, that they will need regional cooperation in Southeast Asia quite as much as we will need it. The bigger Japanese trade and investment in the region become, the more Japan will have to match it with a coherent political policy, if only to forestall a wave of expropriations of her property or restrictions on her trade. The one constructive policy that offers hope of protecting Japan's real national interests in the region, without suggesting Japanese commitments beyond what Japanese public opinion is likely to accept, is the policy of promoting regional cooperation.

3. Each government in Southeast Asia faces grave problems in maintaining internal order; each may be vulnerable to serious internal upheaval, possibly encouraged from without and probably marked with considerable violence. As a result of our experience in Vietnam, we know that the United States cannot take direct responsibility for internal security in these countries. We do have

it in our power to withhold or supply military equipment and training and to re-enforce or liquidate our military bases. Whether we exercise these powers or not, our actions or inactions will be important factors bearing on the stability of the region. We can exercise them in ways tending to promote regional cooperation.

4. Sufficient economic growth has occurred in virtually all the nations of the region to cause elite groups to make development a primary objective. Their need for outside assistance in progressing toward this objective presents us, as I have said, with the most important, continuing opportunities to promote regional cooperation.

Whether or not we take advantage of these opportunities depends on decisions made in Washington.

DEFENSE AND REGIONAL SECURITY

How the United States redefines its security position in East and Southeast Asia will determine in vitally important ways the extent of our influence as a promoter of regional cooperation. This is a vast problem, involving technical considerations of military science well outside my experience. As a development banker, I am naturally most familiar and concerned with the problems and opportunities of development finance. However, it seems plain that if we consider the problems of military bases and military aid simply in narrow, military terms, we are likely to eliminate many opportunities for effective diplomatic action. In fact, if the promotion of regional co-operation is to be a primary objective of foreign policy, it must be a primary objective in any redefinition of our defense posture, as well.

For example, it will no doubt be in our interests at some point to consider renewing our guarantees to Southeast Asia against overt aggression by Red China. Most diplomats with whom I have talked, Americans and Asians alike, believe that the South-East Asia Treaty Organization (SEATO), which has provided the legal basis for our intervention in Vietnam, has little, if any, future. Nor have I yet found an American diplomat familiar with Southeast Asia who thinks that a functioning, regional security organization to take the place of SEATO will be possible within the next decade, at least. However, Australia and New Zealand have rejected isolationism in favor of extending guarantees of military support to Malaysia and Singapore. Quite aside from our own commitments to Thailand, we can hardly avoid some sort of statement of common strategic interests with Australia and New Zealand; they are our partners in the ANZUS pact, and to declare that treaty a dead letter would have implications that no responsible American official, in my opinion, would willingly accept.

Into this difficult and delicate situation, I think it important to insert the objective of promoting regional co-operation. This does not mean coercing the nations of

Southeast Asia into some new military alliance. It does mean consulting with them informally and together about the future of our military bases and future military aid and training. It does mean trying to make any new strategic commitment on our part as much a joint venture as possible.

Informal consultations on defense matters are now going on from time to time among top leaders in the region, especially among the members of ASEAN. That organization's potential usefulness lies in the fact that it has no Western connection—no connection outside the region at all, in fact. This we should respect. If the United States suddenly envisions ASEAN as an integral unit in its own strategic deployment, it will destroy the organization forthwith. However, we can talk informally in other ways with the leaders of the region about our own defense intentions. For example, we might explore with them the possibility of eventually turning over one or more installations in the Philippines to some Southeast Asian organization for the training of Southeast Asia's own military forces. Such a possibility may be a long way off, but introducing the idea now might serve the dual purpose of making our military presence in the Philippines less tendentious, while at the same time offering an earnest of our intent to deploy our military forces in ways tending to encourage regional cooperation and on terms acceptable to the nations of the region.

If we are to abandon counterinsurgency operations engineered largely by ourselves, as I think we should, the problem of maintaining internal stability will remain the number one preoccupation of most governments. It is not a question of maintaining law and order as we talk about it here at home. It is the much more fundamental question of an orderly evolution of legal and political forms of government where all interests are represented. The United States can do very little about this evolution directly, and we should abandon the pretense that we can. However, we must avoid preventing such an evolution, and our ability to furnish or withhold military equipment and training, whether we exercise it or not, is bound to have some bearing on this matter. We cannot simply ignore the fact that these governments will want to buy arms and re-equip their armies from time to time. We cannot safely adopt the attitude that they should stop buying arms and use the money instead for development; the sad case of Malaysia's purchase of ten obsolescent fighter aircraft, to which I referred earlier, is just one illustration of the inadequacy of this kind of posture. In addition to suggesting the possibility that one or more of our military installations in the Philippines might eventually become a base for regional cooperation in military training, we could also, perhaps, encourage the governments of the region to inform each other, through some suitable, formal mechanism, when they intend to buy arms. The facts become well known very quickly, in any case. A ritual of formal notice might mitigate suspicions and place some brake on a desire to buy arms simply to threaten a neighbor.

Intraregional disputes, like that between the Philippines and Malaysia over the state of Sabah, pose the most difficult problems of all for U.S. diplomacy. Prudence tells us to give this sort of dispute the widest possible berth, but our inaction can be as partisan as our actions. We need to devise ways of inhibiting such disputes while not taking sides. Possibly, we and others could encourage the governments involved to seek rituals of mediation, including, perhaps, a sort of Taft-Hartley cooling-off period before there is a resort to threats of armed conflict. The world ought to be inventive enough to offer suitable means of mediation, through the World Court or elsewhere, or to offer a suitable means for rendering good offices to the governments of Southeast Asia in these troublesome cases. The United States may not be able to do more than pay the costs of the rituals, but it would be worth that cost to be able to exert some constructive influence in this direction.

The United States and Japan

The immediate test of our post-Vietnam policy in Asia will, of course, involve our relations with Japan. I see grave danger in talking with Japan about such immediate problems as Okinawa and the U.S.–Japan security treaty solely in the context of short-term strategic interests. As I write, Japanese Foreign Minister Kiichi Aichi and U.S. Secretary of State William P. Rogers are opening negotiations expected to last several months. In my view, the worst mistake we could make would be to so concentrate our interests in these negotiations on the fact that Japan is spending on its own defense only 1 per cent of its substantial gross national product as to risk making U.S. pressure the excuse that the Japanese Government uses to begin rearmament. I am convinced that it is very much in our interests to grant to the Japanese the time they need to define for themselves a new role in the world. A premature decision, exacted as a result of U.S. impatience or pressure, could bring disastrous results inside Japan over the next several years.

If the United States conducts these negotiations in the context of a policy designed to promote regional cooperation in Southeast Asia, it is at least possible that the Japanese will, of their own accord and not as a *quid pro quo* for the reversion of Okinawa or some similar concession on our part, respond by devoting more effort and resources to that end. Insofar as the Japanese themselves see investment in development in Asia as an alternative to investment in rearmament, it surely is in our best interests to encourage that approach.

The Japanese remain a very practical people. I cannot believe that any Japanese Government in the foreseeable future is going to be blind to the common strategic interests our two countries have in East Asia, even if Japanese public opinion is not likely to be very understanding of these matters. For example, surely no Japanese Government is going to want to see the United States prevented from coming to the military aid of South Korea or Taiwan, should that be necessary; a military vacuum in this area would be a serious threat to Japan.

I take it for granted that Japan will sometime again become a major arms producer. Perhaps this will occur as a result of the needs of the Southeast Asian nations to re-equip their armies. Such needs could be rationalized in Japan simply as a good, commercial proposition. I would not rule out such a development as being in the U.S. interest. However, the important thing is to allow as much time as possible for the Japanese themselves to decide such matters with as little provocation as possible from the United States. We must not underestimate the desire of the Japanese to find a new relationship of equality with us to replace a relationship that they have come to regard as subservient.

We should use that time which the Japanese must have to accentuate our own peaceful interests in promoting regional cooperation and to involve the Pacific community in that task. To this end, there is room for a new medium of political exchange between our two countries. Although the business communities of the United States and Japan have established a growing number of connections, formal and informal, and although on matters of trade and economic policy our two governments exchange views regularly at the Cabinet level, there is not yet anything like the kind of political exchange that characterizes our relations with our European allies. This defect should be corrected.

Shortly after World War II, Prince Bernhard of the Netherlands formed an organization called the Bilderberg Group, which brought together prominent people from government and private life from both sides of the Atlantic to discuss, privately and without press coverage, fundamental problems affecting the Atlantic community. I attended several meetings of this group over the years, got to know many important people, and heard many points of view that I might not otherwise have understood. The organization had no official standing; its meetings were always informal. I think it would be a very good idea if some such high-level, unofficial organization were formed to bring together important people from the Pacific community of nations at this time. This should not be an American initiative; it would be very good if it could be a Japanese initiative. But the important thing is to provide a means whereby political problems affecting the Pacific community could be talked out in private among those whose attitudes and actions will be influential. In this way, perhaps, some potentially serious misunderstandings within the Pacific region could be corrected before they have a chance to grow into serious impediments to cooperation.

A New Approach to Foreign Aid

Because our foreign aid program has been so thoroughly and, I think, so tragically identified with the Vietnam war, a major policy consideration affecting our future role in Southeast Asia involves deciding what the future of this branch of U.S. diplomacy should be. In earlier chapters, I have suggested a few of the channels open to us to use development assistance to encourage regional cooperation. These suggestioins have one thing in common: they envisage channeling much more development assistance through regional and international organizations like the World Bank and the Asian Development Bank. This is one key to the kind of policy reform I believe is urgently needed.

At this writing, foreign aid threatens to become a major institutional casualty of the war. The once robust public and professional support for foreign aid has largely evaporated. No piece of legislation causes more irritation and frustration in Congress than the annual foreign aid bill. Among the public, a great cloud of indifference has descended on the subject.

Unlike many who dwell upon the waste and inefficiency that has been one characteristic of our foreign aid program,

I think it has been, on the whole, a success. One can always point to crises that occur despite foreign aid, but it is very difficult to spot those that do not occur, perhaps because of foreign aid. That there has been no serious outbreak of famine in the world for a long time now is a fact, and our foreign aid program helped to make it a fact. That there has been an historically unprecedented rate of economic growth in Latin America, Asia, and Africa over the past decade is a fact, and our aid helped to make it a fact.

However, quite aside from the loss of public support, I think the program, as it has operated in recent years, has suffered serious weaknesses. I think we have concentrated too little on quality, that is, development, and too much on quantity, that is, economic growth. Furthermore, as Congress has become increasingly disillusioned, it has condemned the administrators of foreign aid to a legislative incarceration so confining, so set about with the fetters of red tape, that I find it amazing that the machinery of AID functions at all. I have great sympathy for the men who have tried to make the program effective in these increasingly difficult circumstances, especially David Bell, William Gaud, and Rutherford Poats, with all of whom I have worked closely. But then I have just as much sympathy for Congress, presented as it has been year after year with lists of new programs, new activities, new looks, new gimmicks, many of which were designed not to illuminate the real opportunities and the real difficulties in development finance, but rather to preserve the old rationales and to keep the old bureaucratic machinery turning over for one more year.

We need a new rationale for foreign aid and a new means of practicing development diplomacy. Since the world has come to identify our foreign aid program so much with events in Southeast Asia, and since I believe development finance should play a central role in our policy after the cessation of hostilities in Vietnam, it is logical to discuss a reform in foreign aid in the context of a new policy in Southeast Asia.

Ten years hence, say, I personally would like to see most of what we call foreign aid channeled through international or regional banks or funds. I think it is going to be less and less possible for the United States to exercise economic power through bilateral foreign aid, even if this were deemed desirable. The more that other governments learn the rudiments of development finance, the less they are going to accept our participation in their domestic policy decisions. Nor is such participation necessarily desirable even if it can be made temporarily acceptable. I question whether the scale or the character of bilateral intervention that has characterized our foreign aid program in the past any longer represents a real national interest.

As a development banker, I am frankly a partisan of

multilateral and regional organizations, partly because while President of the World Bank I learned how effective they can be and partly because it is possible in such organizations to insulate the business of development finance somewhat from the competing and conflicting interests that beset all national governments. Those who lend money against long term repayment have to take a long view; they make deals which, if they are good deals, have to survive the ups and downs of commercial and diplomatic intercourse. If the credit supply is turned on and off like a water faucet, there can never be that degree of confidence between borrower and lender on which successful development finance depends. Standards have to be set; they have to be negotiated with sovereign governments in widely differing cultural environments. The negotiations often involve sensitive issues in the domestic affairs of borrowing governments. It stands to reason that this kind of intervention will be more acceptable if it comes from organizations where both the lenders and the borrowers are among the "owners," if you will. Or to put it the other way around, it does not stand to reason that the U.S. Government should undertake in the name of development to intervene wholesale in the domestic affairs of six dozen or so poor countries.

There are other reasons for my partisanship. An international or regional bank or fund can draw on the capital resources and the human resourcefulness of many nations.

An ability to draw on many sources of capital, not just one, is the best way I know to increase the supply of capital for development assistance, and an ability to draw talent from many nations, not just one, is a great asset, for no one nation has a monopoly on the skills needed for effective development finance.

The international bureaucracy, like our own, grew like Topsy at a time when utopian ideas of the possibilities of wholesale intervention in the name of development held sway. As a result, the U.N. system, particularly, is something of an administrative nightmare, which urgently demands the application of good management standards. It should be an important part of our "development diplomacy," and that of other rich countries as well, to use our influence to improve the performance and the management of these organizations. I think the best way of doing this is to adopt a policy of gradually shifting our own development assistance from bilateral to multilateral channels. By using our influence to strengthen international and regional development organizations, we will be broadening and deepening that one area of international cooperation which offers the best hope for gaining acceptance among the many diverse nations of the world community.

A world dedicated to development is, in my view, a necessary prerequisite to a world at peace or a world in which law has some real force.

Partly because the United States will always have special national reasons for providing development assistance, partly because of the limits of the international bureaucracy's effectiveness, we will probably always have to have a bilateral assistance program of our own. It should be lodged in a permanent institution, and it should reflect some of the lessons we have learned, not only in Vietnam but elsewhere during the experience of our several foreign aid programs.

I cannot believe, for one thing, that we should charge to foreign aid, as we do now, and ask a U.S. development agency to administer, as we do now, funds appropriated to further the immediate, short-range objectives of American foreign policy, such as the Vietnam war, or of counterinsurgency operations, such as police training programs. These may from time to time be necessary, but they have nothing to do with development finance, and Congress should be presented with separate legislative requests for their support. The State Department and the Pentagon should be responsible for administering such unusual foreign-policy-support programs; they should be clearly labeled as temporary. Congress has a right, indeed a duty, to judge such requests separately and on the merits of the case, not as a part of a package mislabeled foreign aid. There would be more understanding of and support for foreign policy in Congress if less were camouflaged as foreign aid, and more support for foreign aid in Congress if development assistance were disentangled from matters of foreign policy to which it is not relevant.

This is another way of saying that I think our bilateral assistance program should have its own bureaucratic home. That home should be a bank or a fund, not an annex of the State Department. I think President Nixon should consider asking the Congress to establish a separate fund, say with $3 billion in initial capital, as the financial and administrative expression of the U.S. bilateral assistance program. Such a fund would be replenished, not every year, but only as the need arose. Congress, when it is not considering an appropriation request, could then concentrate on reviewing and evaluating performance and strengthening management and personnel practices.

Unfortunately, as in any banking operation, it is not possible to present Congress in advance of appropriations with a precise description of what development finance is going to be used for. It often takes months, as I have said, to make a deal with a foreign government. Furthermore, the banker-client relationship should be reasonably confidential if development finance is to be effective. Sensitive issues involving the domestic policies of other, sovereign governments are often involved. The present procedures under which AID justifies its requests to the Congress on the basis of illustrative programs are self-defeating. They make subsequent negotiations with foreign governments much more difficult; they stimulate more suspicion than confidence; and they result in actions that bear little resemblance to the illustrations offered in justification for the money in the first place.

New legislation establishing a permanent, separate development assistance fund should indicate that the prime purposes of such a fund would be to finance specific projects and programs in agriculture, education, and public health (the latter especially as it is concerned with family planning) in countries that are prepared to join in the financing of such projects and programs and follow reasonably sound fiscal and monetary policies. In practice, these would not be very confining limitations; they would permit financing virtually every aspect of a Mekong development program, for example. But these limitations would serve to focus attention here and abroad on those most difficult development problems for which bilateral finance, on terms easier than conventional loans, is desperately needed.

It might be worth considering, too, channeling special contributions to international and regional banks through this new fund in order to give more coherence to our development assistance efforts. As long as U.S. bilateral assistance funds are seen, particularly in Congress, as competing with U.S. contributions to international and regional development organizations, undue weight is likely to be given to parochial bureaucratic interests. If Congress set policy in terms of giving priority to the use of international channels, as I think it should, then it would seem wise to me to let the new development fund be the U.S. point of contact with the relevant regional and international development organizations.

Reconciling the State Department's duty to control policy with the demands of efficient management in development finance will always be a tricky problem. The government has tried to solve the problem by putting the development agency inside the State Department. I favor putting it outside the State Department. Neither is a perfect choice. However, whether it is put inside or outside, I do think it important to leave to the State Department the full responsibility for representation overseas. As long as the job of representation abroad is divided among many competing agencies, of which AID is an important example, it will prevent building up within the Foreign Service of the United States those skills which are needed in a modern, professional diplomatic service.

Effective development finance does not require a large, permanent presence on the customer's home ground. In fact, such a presence is, in my view, highly undesirable. The most dangerous consequence was pinpointed recently in a report of the National Planning Association (NPA) of Washington, D.C., entitled, "A New Conception of U.S. Foreign Aid." The authors of the report remark that over the past fifteen years, thanks in part to the success of the U.S. foreign aid program, leaders in most poor countries have accumulated a great deal of knowledge about how to go about encouraging development. But, they go on to say:

> Leadership groups . . . still have difficulty in agreeing on development objectives and assigning a high enough priority to them compared with the other competing national, group, and individual goals. This is a political problem and, while the ability to solve it can be improved by the availability of external assistance, the will to do so cannot be imported. Moreover, an effort to generate the necessary concensus and commitment from outside— particularly by officials of the most powerful nation in the world—tends to exacerbate rather than lessen the problem.

I agree with the authors of the NPA study that, in general, it is not a good thing, especially for resident U.S. officials, to try to influence priorities in the domestic policy of sovereign governments, even in favor of development goals. Insofar as it is in the national interest to undertake this kind of direct intervention anyway, the officials belong in the Foreign Service of the United States, not in a development finance agency. Except in very special cases, resident representatives of development finance agencies should be concerned simply with administrative matters of interest to that agency.

As a rule, technical assistance personnel, employed by the U.S. Government, should also not be stationed overseas for long periods. Many too many today are employed by the U.S. Government who should be employed instead by the governments requiring their services or advice. Too much of what we call technical assistance fails because a man cannot be the hired hand of two governments at once and hope to be effective. Helping others to contract for the technical assistance and advice they need is one of the most important functions of development finance. But the contract should be between those who want assistance and those capable of providing it; the banker, even if he finances the contract indirectly or directly, should stay out of the negotiations. The banker's influence is expressed through the negotiations and the documents involved in the lending process.

If the U.S. Government did more to help others contract for the assistance they need and provided fewer hired hands of its own, and if those AID officials overseas who are performing high-level diplomatic tasks were absorbed into the Foreign Service where they belong, it should be possible gradually to eliminate our permanent bilateral aid missions overseas. By vesting our foreign aid progam in a fund or a bank, managed by a small but highly competent staff, without the encumbrance of large permanent missions overseas, we would be substituting for an overly active policy one that invites others to come to us with their own projects and programs. Our invitation should be as generous as we can make it; I am not recommending a cutback in the funds devoted to foreign aid. But I am suggesting sufficient disengagement overseas to give full play to the importance of self-help in development finance.

The place to start with this kind of reform is Southeast Asia. If the cessation of hostilities in Vietnam leaves the United States with any option, I think we should reduce promptly our AID missions in Saigon and in Thailand and Laos. In any case, these missions, because of their deep involvement in the war, are atypical; their elimination in favor of channeling more assistance through regional and international organizations should be part of the general reduction of the official U.S. presence in Southeast Asia. The U.S. Government, in my view, should help the Vietnamese (and the Thais and the Laos) to contract themselves for the services and advisers they need in the reconstruction period, rather than encouraging them any longer to rely on pesonnel supplied by and working for the United States.

These prescriptions may seem too passive to those who are familiar with the terrible statistics of misery that are used to delineate rich nations from poor nations today. I certainly believe that the United States should be willing to devote 1 per cent of its national income, along with other rich nations, to helping poor nations with their developmental problems, for their poverty makes talk of the subject here at home seem trivial. This target has been advanced for several years now as the measure of a just contribution, but, in fact, the United States has been moving away from it, not toward it. In 1964, we were a leader among the sixteen rich nations offering development assistance; in 1968, we ranked seventh; in 1969, we will rank tenth in terms of the share of our national income devoted to official and private aid. That share is closer to 0.5 per cent of our national income than it is to 1 per cent.

What I conclude from these facts is that the quantitative appeal has not worked. Realization of the seemingly endless suffering on our planet has numbed us, not spurred us to action. This is not surprising. The poor countries of the world embrace a wide variety of particular situations; their collective needs are infinite, while the resources available to help them are limited. In these circumstances, global calculations of the need for capital are of little, if any, practical use. That these targets and calculations of need have not proved effective instruments for rallying public support merely reinforces my belief that development finance must be seen as a quality, not a quantity, business.

This is not to deny that on grounds of justice there should be a greater flow of capital resources from the rich to the poor countries. On the contrary, I would greatly favor, for example, an alteration in the rules of international trade to permit poor countries free and one-way access to the markets of the rich for their exports of manufactured goods, even textiles. The refusal of the rich countries to allow the poor to earn more of their way in the world in this manner is, I believe, a profound injustice. Likewise, if there is need for greater liquidity in the international monetary system, as the rich countries now agree there is, the just way to introduce that new liquidity would be through making it available to poor countries in order to buy more in rich countries.

The channels of development finance, however, are concerned with much more than just transfers of capital. They are concerned with helping the poor countries prepare sound projects and programs, which promise a high return to society. It is not, in the first instance, the limited supply of capital that determines the usefulness of these channels of cooperation; it is the ability of the poor countries to come forward with specific projects and programs that can be financed. If quality standards are not put first, development finance loses its identity and purpose.

Alternative in Southeast Asia

These general remarks on the future of foreign aid have a particular importance for our future role in Southeast Asia. I have been posing an alternative to our present policy of over-involvement in the affairs of these nations. Briefly, that alternative envisions a resurrection of the ancient art of diplomacy and a substitution of cooperation in development for involvement in counterinsurgent warfare. The willingness of Americans to adjust and then re-enforce our foreign aid programs is the most concrete means open to us to show that we have not lost confidence either in ourselves or in our friends in this part of the world. It is the concrete way of showing that when we talk about disengagement we are not merely being defeatist.

The Vietnam war has engendered grave doubts among Americans about their foreign policy. I hope I have shown that I believe we should seriously question some of our actions and attitudes in the recent past. But, if we succumb to these doubts, to a sort of national guilt feeling, we will, I fear, convert our unhappy experience in Vietnam into a catastrophe. It has never been more urgent that we act with confidence, resolution, and wisdom in Southeast Asia than it is today.

The mere invention of activities does not convey confidence, resolution, and wisdom. In fact, we will fail unless we learn how to curb our impulsive acts through the hard disciplines of diplomacy. Because vast forces of history are at work, the normal state of relations among nations can never be one of perfect cooperation. The normal state involves living with competing and conflicting tensions that inevitably prevent nations from adopting the same scale of moral values that individuals can. As a consequence, we have to be sure that our foreign policy ideals are always firmly rooted in real interests, that the moral dimension of policy does not become separated from a rational consideration of the possibilities and limitations of our influence. Only in this kind of context can we give effective expression to our faith in the constructive power of action.

But neither in Southeast Asia nor in any other corner of the globe can U.S. diplomacy look forward to a period of inactive recuperation. All over the world, and particularly in Southeast Asia, leaders are talking to one another as never before. In Southeast Asia, particularly, there is a common awareness of regional problems and opportunities that few would have dared believe possible even a decade ago. Whether one chooses to say that this new awareness is the result of the success or the failure of U.S. diplomacy is really beside the point. What is undeniable is that the actions of the United States have been one of the most important reasons, if not the most important reason, for the great changes that have come about. We can no more run away from this fact than a man can run away from his parentage. Either we come to terms with the impact of our heritage or we condemn ourselves to self-destruction.

I believe there is a salvation for nations, as for individuals, in work. I know there is a world of work to be done. The vision of a developed Mekong basin is a good example of the sort of work with which the United States ought to be identified. It is work that inhibits violence and chaos. It inculcates habits of cooperation. It provides a healthy outlet for American inventiveness. It brilliantly illustrates the infinite possibilities that lie hidden in the idea of development. Sobered by our experience in Vietnam, but neither ashamed nor frightened, most Americans today, whatever the generation gap and the stresses that divide us, will agree, I think, that it is important for us to engage a measure of our talent and resources in just such work. This is the good that can live on in the new era of foreign policy we are entering and not be buried with the past.